WABI-SABI
SEWING

20 sewing patterns for perfectly imperfect projects

Karen Lewis

sewandso

www.sewandso.co.uk

CONTENTS

10

58

74

28

36

106

96

64

44

18

52

100

86

78

14

40

70

48

92

24

INTRODUCTION

I have always been drawn to scrappy quilts and textiles, the irregularity of hand printing, mix and-match pottery, the beauty of something not being quite perfect. To me, these elements give objects character and personality. In wabi-sabi terms, those objects are perfectly imperfect.

Wabi-sabi is a Japanese aesthetic ethos that focuses on the imperfect in a positive way, embracing natural imperfections. But, what does wabi-sabi mean to today's crafters? To me, it evokes the idea of using the fabric we already have and using a bit of this and that when we run short, celebrating the results of hunting down mismatched yet treasured scraps. My log cabin quilt makes a feature of incorporating a splash of red where the lengths of blue fabric weren't quite long enough. The flying geese in the placemats don't all have to be the same. Grab what fabric you have and see the character come to life with the addition of an unexpected piece.

The variety of fabrics in my projects evokes the wabi-sabi ethos: linens and barkcloth with their textural weave; hand printed fabrics oozing with the character of the artist's hand; hand dyed fabrics adding depth and charm with uneven colour.

Hand stitching is a clever way to showcase wabi-sabi. Not only do these stitches vary with each one (well mine do!) but hand sewing one stitch at a time embraces every step of the process. I have paid homage to sashiko stitching as well as simple running stitches. Sashiko is a precise, traditional Japanese embroidery method originally used for repairs. Today it is used as a decorative stitch, and within the aesthetic of wabi-sabi, I have employed a more freeform style.

Visible mending is an aspect of today's make-do-and-mend approach that to me is authentically wabi-sabi. What could be truer than embracing the wear and tear of a much used and loved item through its repair? The treatment of the jeans in the visible mending project can be incorporated into any manner of worn items to embrace them in a decorative way.

Wabi-sabi suits me. My stitches aren't always even. My seams aren't always straight. But I embrace the character of the fabrics and imperfections, and I hope you will too. Most of these projects are designed from the starting point 'use what you have'. You don't need matchy matchy brand-new fabrics. Your favourite pieces, no matter how small, will be full of character and perfect for your project. Or in the words of wabi-sabi... perfectly imperfect.

TOOLS & MATERIALS

This book doesn't use any particularly fancy or special equipment. When it comes to fabric, these projects are an excellent excuse to raid your fabric stash and use up all those special scraps you've been saving for a rainy day!

ESSENTIAL TOOLS

- Sewing machine: You need a ¼in seam foot, and a zipper foot for any project that includes a zipper.
- Thread: Use a good quality neutral 100% cotton thread for both machine and hand piecing. I love Aurifil 50 for its quality and colour selection.
- Pins: For both piecing and basting. Glass-head pins look pretty, and normally a pin that goes to extra lengths to look good is also high quality!
- Scissors: Fabric shears, small sharp embroidery scissors, and paper scissors for cutting templates.
- Self-healing cutting mat: The biggest one you can afford and have space to accommodate.
- Rotary cutter and spare blades: Essential for cutting patchwork fabric. Again, get the best you can afford; I like an Olfa with its easy-to-change blade.
- Quilting rulers: A non-slip 6in x 24in ruler with angles and ⅛in markings is my choice, along with a small ruler, and a square for trimming blocks.
- Fabric pencil: For marking quilting and templates, and making removeable marks on fabric.
- Embroidery thread: For hand quilting and sashiko stitching I use Aurifil 12 or Aurifil Lana wool which adds a beautiful texture to your stitches. Lana wool isn't as hard wearing, so be mindful if you are using it for an item that will be heavily used or washed.
- Hand sewing needles: My needle of choice is Jeana Kimball's Embroidery/Redwork size 9. It is long and super sharp. Traditionally hand quilting needles are shorter but I prefer a longer needle.
- Basting pins/basting spray: I find basting my quilts preferable with a spray; I use 505 Adhesive.
- Seam ripper: Every sewist's best friend!
- Iron and ironing board: Preferably a steam iron to smooth out creases in your fabric.

MATERIALS

- For piecing: I have used a variety of quilting cotton, denim, linen, double gauze and barkcloth in my projects. I love the textures that a variety of different weight fabrics give, and mixing them together in a project adds pleasing interest. I have also used hand printed and hand dyed fabric, both of which glow in handmade pieces.
- Wadding (batting): My favourite wadding is Heirloom Premium Cotton for no other reason than I can buy it in a big roll! It does have a nice soft feel, and the cotton is natural and breathable. You can use a thinner wadding for wall quilts.
- Ribbon: As this is used for tie-fastenings and closures, choose a type that is hard wearing enough not to fray.

SPECIALIST TOOLS & MATERIALS

The following make hooks and handles for various projects in the book. They add a professional touch, but fabric alternatives are always available!

- Rivets and rivet tool
- Eyelets and eyelet tool
- Leather strapping

LIVING

What better way to introduce wabi-sabi to your life than through your everyday living space. Nestle in with a cushion or quilt, put your feet up, place your mug on a coaster, and admire some handmade wall art. Let the ethos of 'perfectly imperfect' reign all around.

Hexagon Harmony

FINISHED SIZE: 14in x 22in

I have started many English Paper Piecing (EPP) projects, only to run out of time. This cushion is the answer – big enough to get your teeth into without losing sight of the finish line! The other big plus is that you can use all those tiny scraps you have hoarded away, as no two hexies need to be the same. You will be cuddling up on the sofa with the finished results before you know it.

- -

Materials:

- Approximately ¾yd in total of fabric for the cushion front
- ½yd fabric for the cushion back
- 2½in x 30in for binding
- 18in x 28in wadding (batting)
- Embroidery thread for hand quilting (optional)
- 14in x 20in cushion pad

CUTTING

1 Cut out the fabric as follows:

From the cushion front fabric:
- One hundred and twenty-eight (128) 2½in squares

From the cushion back fabric:
- Two 15in squares

From the binding fabric:
- Two 15in lengths

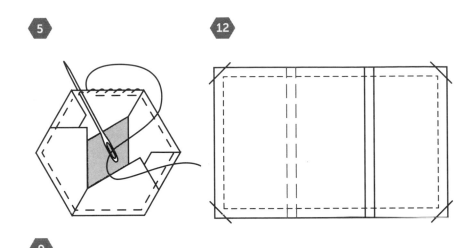

SEWING THE HEXAGONS

2 Make seven copies of the hexagon template page (see Templates) and cut out. You will have one hundred and forty (140) 1in hexagon paper pieces. Put 12 aside as spares or for future projects; you will be left with one hundred and twenty-eight (128) paper pieces.

3 With the 2½in squares of fabric, make one hundred and twenty-eight (128) 1in hexagons (see Techniques: English Paper Piecing). Press the pieces but do not remove the papers yet.

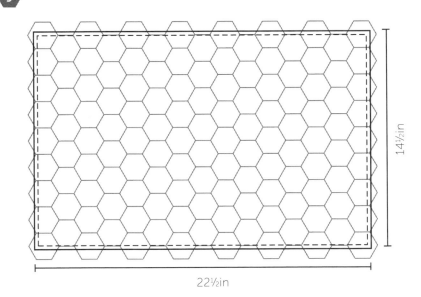

22½in

14½in

ASSEMBLING THE FRONT

4 Arrange your hexagons into eight vertical rows of nine alternated with eight rows of eight.

5 Join the hexagons to create the rows. Place two pieces right sides together, aligning the edges. Using hand-sewn whip stitches, sew the two pieces together along one edge. Try to catch just a few threads of fabric using very small stitches. Don't pull too tight; just enough to ensure the edges meet with no space between. At the end of one side, knot the thread on the back, trim and open out the two hexies. Join the next piece in the same way, and so on.

6 Once you have sewn all the rows together, arrange them in the desired order, remembering to alternate long and short rows. Sew each row to the next, using the same whip stitch as before. You will find that you have to bend and contort the pieces a little as you join the rows. However, the paper you left in will stabilize everything as you work.

7 Press your whole cushion front and then carefully remove all the paper pieces (you should be able to use these again). You don't need to remove the tacking (basting) threads unless they show through on the right side.

QUILTING THE FRONT

8 Spray or pin baste the cushion front onto the piece of wadding (batting) and quilt as desired (see Techniques: Hand Quilting). Since this is a lovely slow hand-stitching project, I hand quilted using random horizontal lines in different colours of embroidery thread.

9 Once quilted, trim the edges to measure 14½in x 22½in.

MAKING THE BACK

10 Sew binding to one short raw edge of each of the back pieces (see Techniques: Binding a Raw Edge).

11 Place the cushion front with the right side up. Position the two backing pieces overlapping to make the cushion's envelope back, with right sides down. The bound edges should be opposite the short edges of the cushion front. Pin these three pieces in place all around the edge and sew together.

12 Clip off each of the four corners to reduce bulk. Turn the cover the right way out and insert your cushion pad to finish.

Picture Imperfect

FINISHED SIZE: 20in x 20in

I love the tranquillity of Hawaiian quilts, with their minimal colour palette and symmetrical botanical motifs. They are normally made from a single piece of appliquéd fabric, but I have added my twist with the addition of separate pieces incorporated into the design. I also swapped the traditional echo quilting for widely spaced sashiko lines. This project resizes easily by enlarging or reducing the templates.

Materials:

- 24in square of background fabric
- 20in square of main motif fabric
- 10in square of flower motif fabric
- 6in square of circle motif fabric
- 24in square of backing fabric
- 24in square of wadding (batting)
- 90in of binding fabric
- Embroidery thread for hand quilting (optional)

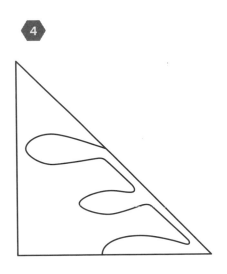

PREPARING THE MOTIFS

1 Photocopy or trace the main, flower and circle motif templates (see Templates) and cut out.

2 Fold the background fabric in half, then in half again. Press to mark the centre point, open up and set aside.

3 With wrong sides together, fold the main motif fabric in half diagonally and half again, making sure the corner points and edges align. Fold one more time then press flat.

4 Pin the main motif template in position on your folded fabric, making sure to pin through all the layers. Draw around the template with a fabric pencil, remove the paper then carefully cut out.

5 Place the flower and circle templates on the wrong side of their corresponding fabrics and pin in place. Draw around with a fabric pencil to create four of each, then cut out.

6 Unfold the main motif piece and press all the motifs flat.

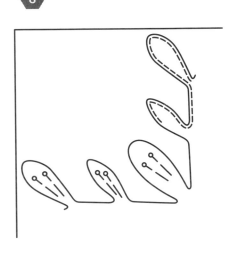

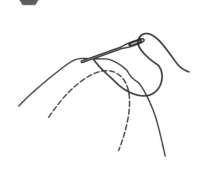

STITCHING THE MOTIFS IN PLACE

7 Pin the main motif onto the background fabric, with both fabrics right sides up. Match the centre points to ensure the motif is aligned correctly on the background.

8 Tack (baste) the motif in place ¼in inside the motif's edge using a ½in running stitch (see Techniques: Running Stitch). Remove the pins and smooth the fabric as you go.

9 Use needle-turn appliqué to stitch the motif in place. To begin, tie a knot in your thread and bring your needle through from the back of the background fabric at one of the corners by the centre of the motif. Turning the raw edge of the motif under ⅛in with the point of your needle as you go, sew small stitches all the way around. When you get to a curved area work your stitches closer together.

10 Once you have appliquéd the main motif in place, refer to the photograph to position and pin the flower motifs in place and appliqué, followed by the circle motifs. Use the same needle-turn appliqué method throughout.

MAKING THE WALL HANGING

11 Make a quilt sandwich with the backing fabric right side down, then the wadding (batting), and your appliquéd piece on top right side up (see Techniques: Making a Quilt Sandwich).

12 Quilt with your preferred quilting method, whether this is hand quilting (see Techniques: Hand Quilting), the traditional Hawaiian style of echo machine-quilting, or another method of your choice. I hand stitched horizontal rows of running stitch 1½in apart.

13 Trim the quilt sandwich to 20in square making sure your appliquéd motifs remain central to your finished piece.

14 Cut two 2½in squares from the end of your binding fabric to make hanging tabs. Fold the squares in half diagonally, wrong side facing, and sew into the top two corners on the back of the hanging

15 Bind the wall hanging to finish (see Techniques: Binding Your Quilt).

Comfort Cubed

FINISHED SIZE: 13in x 22in x 22in

A pouffe is just the place to rest tired legs, put down your tray of coffee and biscuits, and even seat guests. Bold piecing makes it decorative when not in use, with the top designed to look gorgeous from any angle. The top is also a quick sew with the half square triangles (HSTs) made eight at a time! For a hard-wearing finish, the top is quilted and a sturdy denim used for the sides and base.

- -

Materials:

- 5in square of dark-blue fabric for centre (a)
- 5in x 13in of light-blue fabric (b)
- One fat-quarter of yellow fabric (c)
- ¾yd of background fabric (d)
- 1½yds of fabric for sides and base (e)
- 25in square of wadding (batting)
- Embroidery thread for hand quilting (optional)
- 20in zipper
- Four cubic feet of filling of choice (this can be a variety of things from beanbag filling to fabric scraps and wadding (batting) offcuts)

CUTTING

1 Cut out the fabric as follows:

From fabric (a):

- One 4¾in square

From fabric (b):

- Two 3⅞in squares, cut diagonally in half to yield four triangles
- Four 2½in squares

From fabric (c):

- Three 6¾in squares
- Twelve 2½in squares
- Four 2½in x 4½in rectangles

From fabric (d):

- Three 6¾in squares
- Four 2½in squares
- Four 2½in x 4½in rectangles
- Four 2½in x 6½in rectangles
- Two 2½in x 18½in strips
- Two 2½in x 22½in strips

From fabric (e):

- Four 14in x 23in rectangles
- Two 12in x 23in rectangles

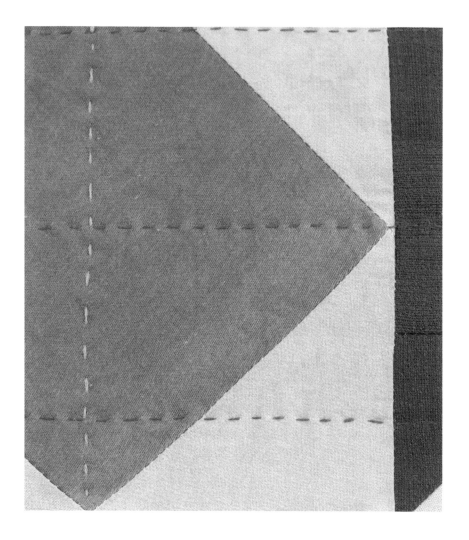

MAKING THE SQUARE-IN-A-SQUARE CENTRE

2 Fold square (a) in half, then half again and gently press to mark the halfway points along each edge.

3 Fold triangles (b) in half along the long side and gently press to mark the halfway point along the edge.

4 Aligning the halfway points and with right sides together, pin and sew a triangle onto the square. Press this open and repeat on the opposite side.

5 Trim the corners by placing your ruler along the edge of the square and then repeat with the other two sides.

6 Press this unit open and trim to 6½in square, making sure you have a ¼in seam allowance on each side of the points.

MAKING THE HALF SQUARE TRIANGLE (HST) UNITS

7 From the three fabric (c) 6¾in squares and three fabric (d) 6¾in squares, make three sets of eight HST units using the Eight-At-a-Time HST method (see Techniques: Half Square Triangles). This will yield twenty-four HST units.

8 Press these units open and trim to 2½in square.

MAKING THE 3 x 3 CORNER UNITS

9 Sew a row of one (b) 2½in square, one (d) 2½in square and one HST.

10 Sew one (d) 2½in x 4½in rectangle onto a (c) 2½in square.

11 Sew a HST onto a (c) 2½in x 4½in rectangle.

12 Press all these strips and sew together to make a 6½in square corner unit. Repeat to make a total of four corner units and press.

MAKING THE 3 x 3 MIDDLE UNITS

13 Sew a row of one (c) 2½in square between two HSTs.

14 Sew a row of one (c) 2½in square between two HSTs.

15 Press both these strips and sew one (d) 2½in x 6½in rectangle between these two. Repeat to make a total of four middle units and press.

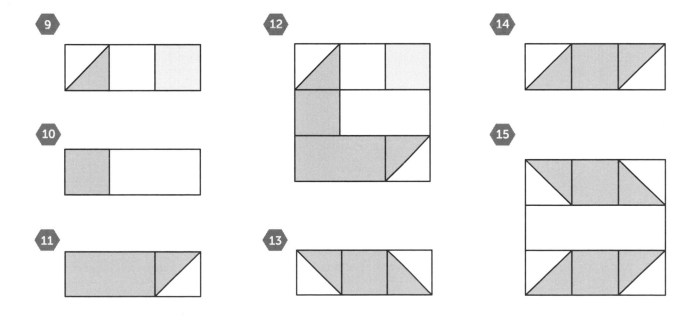

MAKING THE TOP

16 Sew one middle unit between two corner units. Repeat to make two of these rows.

17 Sew the square-in-a-square block between two middle units.

18 Press these three rows and sew together, ensuring the outer rows are facing in the correct direction.

19 Sew fabric (d) 2½in x 18½in strips on the top and the bottom, then press.

20 Sew fabric (d) 2½in x 22½in strips on the left and the right, then press.

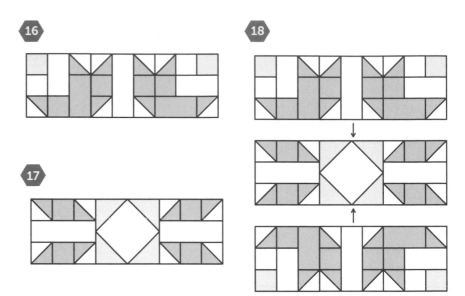

QUILTING THE TOP

21 With right side up, spray or pin baste the pouffe top onto the wadding (batting) and quilt as desired (see Techniques: Hand Quilting). I hand quilted wide straight lines across the top with a running stitch and one vertical line in a contrasting thread.

22 Once quilted, trim the top to 23in square.

ATTACHING THE SIDES TO THE TOP

23 On the back of four pieces of fabric (e), mark a dot ½in in from the corners using a fabric pencil.

24 With right sides together, pin one of these side pieces to the top piece and sew together with a ½in seam allowance, starting and ending just between the dots. Reverse stitch at each end of the seam to strengthen. Repeat for the other three sides of the top.

JOINING THE FOUR SIDES

25 Placing two adjacent side pieces right sides together, pin and sew with a ½in seam allowance. As before, stay between the dots of the side seams. Reverse stitch at each end to strengthen.

26 Repeat for all four side seams. Keep the piece inside out for now.

INSERTING THE ZIPPER

27 Take the two 12in x 23in rectangles of fabric (e) and place right sides together. Along one long edge, sew a seam, reverse stitching a few times for strength at each end no further back than 1½in. Open the two pieces of fabric and with the right sides down press the seam open.

28 Lay your zipper face down on top of the seam, lining the teeth up with the stitched seam and pin in place.

29 With a zipper foot on your machine, sew down one side of the zipper, removing the pins as you go. Stop, with the needle down, just before the end of the zipper and turn to sew across the zipper. Sew back and forth to strengthen, then turn and pivot to sew up the other side of the zipper, again stopping just before the end of the teeth. Open up the zipper halfway and, keeping the teeth touching, sew backwards and forwards across the top of the zipper and finish.

30 Turn the fabric right side up and with a seam ripper remove the stitches to reveal the zipper.

31 Keeping the zipper horizontal and centred, trim the piece to 23in square.

ATTACHING THE BOTTOM TO THE POUFFE AND FINISHING

32 With a fabric pencil, on the back of the bottom piece, mark dots ½in in from the corners as before.

33 Making sure the zipper is open halfway, take this piece and with right sides facing, pin this to one side of the main pouffe. Sew with a ½in seam allowance between the dots, going back and forth at the start and end to strengthen.

34 Repeat with the remaining three sides and then turn right way round through the zipper opening pushing the corners out.

35 Fill with your choice of filling until it is as firm as you would like, then pull the zipper closed.

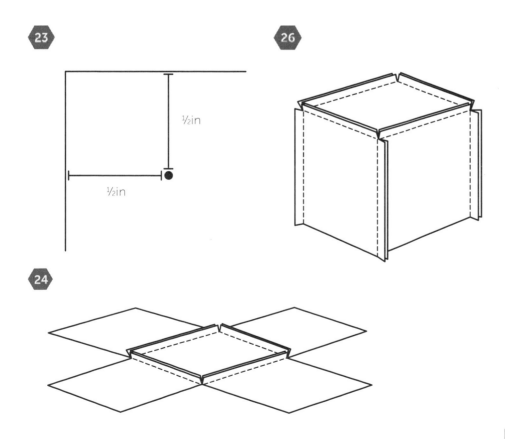

Coasting Gently

FINISHED SIZE: 4½in x 4½in

Mug coasters make a great addition to the table, bringing a subtle touch of colour and design even when not in use. These scrappy coasters can be made from odds and ends of fabrics in your stash, and could even incorporate treasured pieces to show off. I have included instructions to make them double-sided, but you can just use one piece of fabric to make a quick and easy backing if you prefer.

- -

Materials (to make four coasters):

- One fat-sixteenth of front centre fabric
- Eight 4in squares of fabric for the front corners
- One fat-eighth of backing fabric
- 1½in wide fabric scraps for the scrappy back strips (optional)
- 8in square of wadding (batting)
- 8in length of braid for decorative tag (optional)
- Embroidery thread for hand quilting (optional)

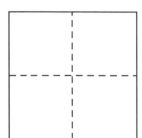

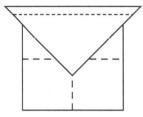

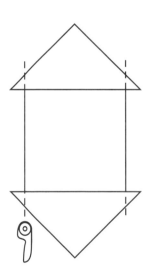

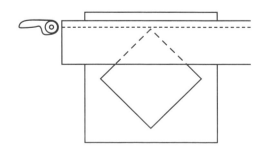

CUTTING

1 Cut out the fabric as follows:

From the front centre fabric:

- Four 3½in squares

From the backing fabric:

- Four 4¾in squares

From the eight 4in squares:

- Cut in half diagonally to create sixteen triangles of front corner fabric

From the wadding (batting):

- Cut four 4in squares

From the braid (optional):

- Cut into four 2in lengths

COASTER FRONT

2 Mix and match the sixteen front corner triangles between the four front centre squares to create your desired combinations.

3 Lightly fold one of the front centre squares in half and half again. These will be your guide lines for making sure the triangles are central.

4 With right sides facing, align the tip of one of the front corner triangles with the vertical fold line on the front centre square and sew in place. Press open and repeat on the opposite side. Trim along the sides of the square and then attach the remaining two triangles.

5 Trim the coaster front to 4¾in square with a seam allowance of ¼in. Do this by placing your ruler ¼in above each corner of the front centre square and cut.

6 Repeat for the remaining three coaster fronts.

COASTER BACK

7 If you are including the optional scrappy strip detail on the coaster back, sew three 1½in wide strips together and trim to make a total length of 4¾in. Cut one of the backing squares into two irregular rectangles and sew the scrappy strip between the two pieces. Trim to 4¾in square with a seam allowance of ¼in.

8 Repeat for the remaining three coaster backs.

MAKING UP

9 With right sides facing, pin the front and back squares together. If you are adding the decorative tag, fold a 2in length of braid in half and position in between the front and back layers with the folded edge of the tag inside.

10 Sew around the four sides leaving a 2in gap for turning.

11 Snip across each corner to avoid bulk and then turn right sides out.

12 Press the coaster, folding the unsewn section of fabric inwards. Push the wadding (batting) through the gap, flattening it out as you go. Sew around the edge of the coaster to close up the gap and create a neat finish.

13 Hand or machine quilt around the square to secure the wadding (batting) in place and add a decorative finish to your coaster.

14 Repeat with the remaining three coasters. Then put your feet up and enjoy a cup of tea!

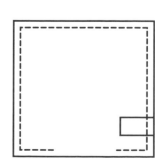

Scattered Stars

FINISHED SIZE: 46in x 60in

Snuggling under a quilt during the day has to be the ultimate in luxury, and this starry quilt is the perfect size to do just that. I love my lap quilts to be low-key in colour and restful on the eye to enhance relaxation. Here, I raided my low-volume stash and paired it with a hand-dyed solid mustard fabric in different depths to provide subtle interest. The rippled star design and hand quilting are equally design-led, yet laid back.

Materials:

- One fat-quarter of solid fabric for the Centre-Star Row
- ½yd of solid fabric for Rows 1 and 2
- One fat-quarter of solid fabric for Row 3
- 3yds in total of low-volume fabric for the background
- 3yds of fabric for backing
- 55in x 70in of wadding (batting)
- ½yd of binding fabric
- Embroidery thread for hand quilting (optional)

CUTTING

1 Cut out the fabric as follows:

From the Centre-Star Row solid fabric:

- Three 7¼in squares
- Six 4in squares

From the Row 1 and Row 2 solid fabric:

- Three 7¼in squares
- Two 3½in x 6½in rectangles
- Ten 4in squares

From the Row 3 solid fabric:

- Three 7¼in squares
- Six 4in squares

From the background fabric:

- Two hundred and four (204) 3½in squares
- Thirty-six 3⅞in squares
- Twenty-two 4in squares

From the backing fabric:

- Two 1½yds x 35in rectangles

MAKING THE CENTRE-STAR ROW

2 From the three 7¼in squares and twelve of the 3⅞in background squares, make three sets of Four-At-a-Time Flying Geese (see Techniques: Flying Geese). This will yield twelve flying geese units.

3 From the six 4in centre-star fabric squares and six 4in background squares, make six pairs of HST units (see Techniques: Half Square Triangles).

4 Sew each of the four centre-star rows together, alternating the prepared units with a total of twenty-eight 3½in background squares.

5 Sew these four rows to each other.

MAKING ROW 1 AND ROW 2

6 From the three 7¼in squares and twelve of the background 3⅞in squares, make three sets of Four-At-a-Time Flying Geese (see Techniques: Flying Geese). This will yield twelve flying geese units.

7 From the two 3½in x 6½in rectangles paired with four of the 3½in background squares, make two traditionally pieced flying geese units (see Techniques: Flying Geese). You will now have 14 flying geese units in total.

8 From the ten 4in squares together with ten background 4in squares, make ten sets of HST pairs (see Techniques: Half Square Triangles).

9 Sew these units together with a total of sixteen 3½in background squares to make four rows of sixteen squares (two each of Row 1 and Row 2).

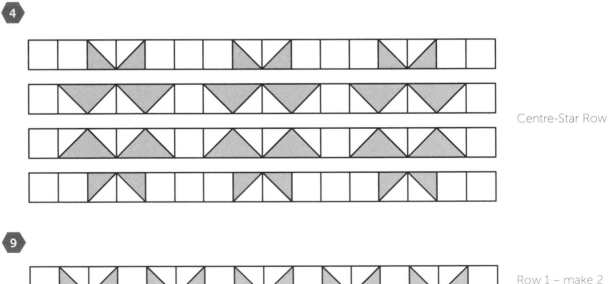

Centre-Star Row

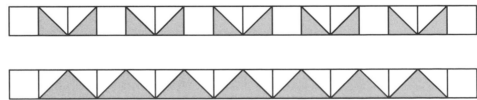

Row 1 – make 2

Row 2 – make 2

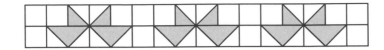

Row 3 –
make 2

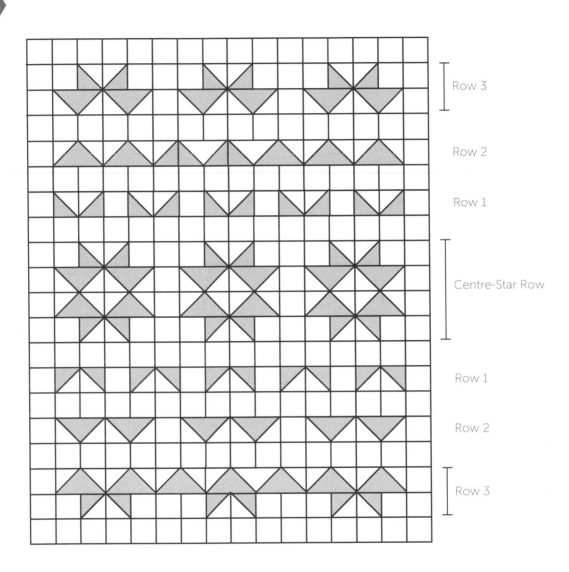

Row 3

Row 2

Row 1

Centre-Star Row

Row 1

Row 2

Row 3

MAKING ROW 3

10 From the three 7¼in squares and twelve background 3⅞in squares, make three sets of Four-At-a-Time Flying Geese (see Techniques: Flying Geese). This will yield twelve flying geese units.

11 From the six 4in squares together with six background 4in squares, make six pairs of HST units.

12 Sew these blocks together with a total of twenty-eight 3½in background squares to make four rows, and then sew two pairs of two rows together.

ASSEMBLING THE QUILT TOP

13 Make eight rows of sixteen 3½in background squares.

14 Sew all the rows together using the diagram as a guide.

QUILTING AND FINISHING

15 Sew the two pieces of backing fabric together along the long sides with a ½in seam allowance. Press the seam open.

16 Make a quilt sandwich with the backing fabric right side down, wadding (batting) and your pieced top right side up (see Techniques: Making a Quilt Sandwich).

17 Quilt with your preferred quilting method; you may choose to hand quilt, machine quilt or use another method of your choice. I used embroidery thread to hand quilt sections echoing the different shapes, combined with some straight-line quilting in between the rows.

18 Trim the quilted sandwich to 46in x 60in.

19 Bind the quilt to finish, taking care to mitre the corners neatly (see Techniques: Binding Your Quilt).

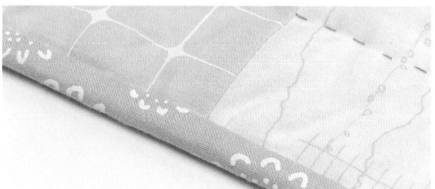

Tip

Make a feature of your hand quilting – mix up the colour of your thread to highlight different areas of the quilt.

EATING

Mealtimes mean family time, so the kitchen is the perfect place to share your love of wabi-sabi with loved ones. Aprons, placemats, and other dining and cooking related linens are such humble objects, and so the perfect canvas for this authentic, charming treatment.

Calm Crossing

FINISHED SIZE: Up to 38in bust

I spend a lot of time in an apron, so a crossover Japanese-style apron that feels more like a dress is perfect. This design uses the full width of fabric from the bolt, so no fiddly measuring. The open back means one size fits all, but you can adjust the straps accordingly. A full yard was the perfect length for me, but measure from under your arm to the desired length to customize.

- -

Materials:

- 1yd linen, cotton or other light fabric (denim is too heavy for this style of apron). If you need more than a yard for the length, don't forget to add 1½in for seam allowances
- ½yd matching or contrasting fabric for the pockets and straps
- 1in x 3in rectangle of fabric for pocket tag (optional)

CUTTING

1 From the matching/contrasting fabric, cut out as follows:

- Two 8in x 22in rectangles for the straps
- Two 8½in x 11in rectangles for the pockets

THE APRON BODY

2 Square up the fabric, removing the selvedge edges. Then starting with the sides, fold the edges inwards ¼in to the wrong side and press. Repeat to hide the raw edge. Sew along both of these edges.

3 Fold the top edge inwards 1in to the wrong side and press. Repeat to hide the raw edge. Sew along this edge.

4 Fold the bottom edge inwards ¼in to the wrong side and press. Repeat to hide the raw edge. Sew along this edge.

MAKING THE STRAPS

5 On each strap piece, fold the short ends inwards ¼in to the wrong side and press. Sew along these folds.

6 Fold each strap piece in half lengthways to the wrong side and press. Open up and fold each half into the middle pressed line to the wrong side so that they meet. Press into position. Fold each piece in half to the wrong side along the initial pressed middle line.

7 Sew along both long edges of each strap as close to the edge as you can.

ATTACHING THE STRAPS

8 Fold the top edge of the apron in half and lightly press to mark the midpoint.

9 Pin one end of each strap on the wrong side of the apron body, 4in from the midpoint of the apron. The right side of each strap should face the wrong side of the apron. The two straps should be a total of 8in apart, and overlapping the apron by 1½in.

10 From the back of the apron sew around all three sides of each overlapping strap end and across the top of the body to secure. You should have two rectangles of stitching.

11 Pin the other ends of the straps to the back of the apron. They should cross over at the back, so the strap on the front right goes to the back left and the strap on the front left goes to the back right. The right side of each strap should face the wrong side of the apron. Pin each end onto the apron ½in from the side edges, overlapping by 1½in, and sew in place.

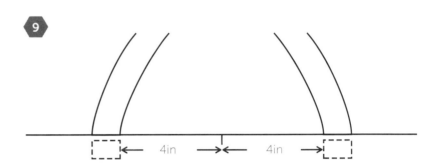

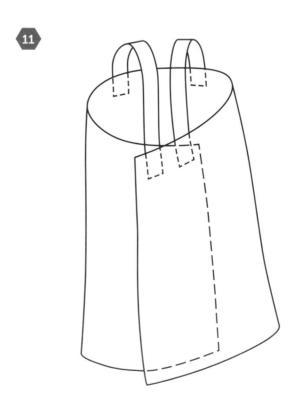

MAKING THE POCKETS

12 Starting with the longer sides, fold the edges inwards ¼in to the wrong side and press firmly.

13 Repeat with the bottom edge, again pressing firmly.

14 Fold the top edge inwards ¼in to the wrong side and press. Repeat to hide the raw edge. Sew along this edge.

15 If adding the pocket tag, take the 1in x 3in rectangle and with wrong sides facing, fold the short edges under ¼in and sew in place. With wrong sides facing, fold and press down the long edge.

ATTACHING THE POCKETS

16 Put on your apron to see where the pockets should be. For me the top of each is approximately 13in down from the top edge of the apron, allowing me to reach inside to the bottom of the pockets. Each pocket is 2½in out from the centre, leaving a total of 5in between the two.

17 Once you are happy with the position, pin the pockets in place. Position the tag 1in from the bottom outside edge of one of the pockets, and pin in place. Sew around the three sides, leaving the top open. Make sure to go forwards and backwards several times at the top of each side to strengthen the seam.

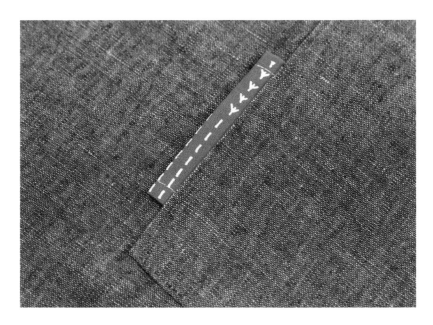

Helping Hands

FINISHED SIZE: 8½in x 8½in

I love a quick-sew project when I'm short of time, and this little project is an instant pick-me-up using treasured scraps. Adding a leather hanging loop to each pot holder creates an extra organic touch and makes the pair a great gift. For practical makes like this, often destined for the kitchen or dining-table, insulating wadding (batting) is a handy standby for your stash.

- -

Materials (to make one pair):

- ½yd of main fabric
- Two 1½in squares for the cross centres
- 6in x 8in rectangle for the cross arms
- Two 6½in x 8½in rectangles for the front linings
- One fat-quarter of insulating wadding (batting)
- Two ½in eyelets
- Two 8in leather ties (optional)

CUTTING

1 Following the layout diagram, cut out the fabric as follows:

From the main fabric:

- Four 8½in squares
- Eight 3in x 4in rectangles
- Two strips 2½in x WOF, cutting one 8½in piece from each and leaving the remaining lengths uncut (these will be the binding)

From the fabric for the cross arms:

- Four 1½in x 4in strips
- Four 1½in x 3in strips

From the wadding (batting):

- Two 8½in squares
- Two 6½in x 8½in rectangles

MAKING THE FRONT

2 With right sides together, sew one 1½in x 3in cross arm between two of the 3in x 4in main fabric rectangles. Repeat to make an identical piece.

3 With right sides together sew the 1½in x 1½in cross centre between two of the 1½in x 4in cross arms.

4 Sew the three pieces together as shown and press.

5 Make a quilt sandwich with the 6½in x 8½in front lining piece, the 6½in x 8½in wadding (batting) and your pieced front; quilt as desired. I quilted a simple design, echoing the cross.

6 Take one of the 2½in x 8½in strips and make binding with it (see Techniques: Binding Your Quilt). Bind the long top edge of your pot holder front.

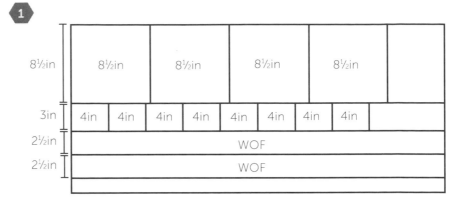

MAKING THE BACK

7 Make a quilt sandwich with two of the 8½in squares of main fabric and the 8½in square of wadding (batting); quilt as desired. Again, I kept the quilting simple and echoed the cross.

MAKING UP THE POT HOLDER

8 With lining sides facing, pin together the pot holder front and back with the lower edge of each aligned.

9 Having turned the longer 2½in strip into binding (see Techniques: Preparing the Binding), bind all the way around the pot holder.

10 Following the manufacturer's instructions, attach an eyelet to one corner of your pot holder and thread the leather tie through to make a hanger. You can knot the leather, or add a rivet. Alternatively, leave out the leather and use the eyelet as your hanger.

11 Repeat the steps above to make the second pot holder.

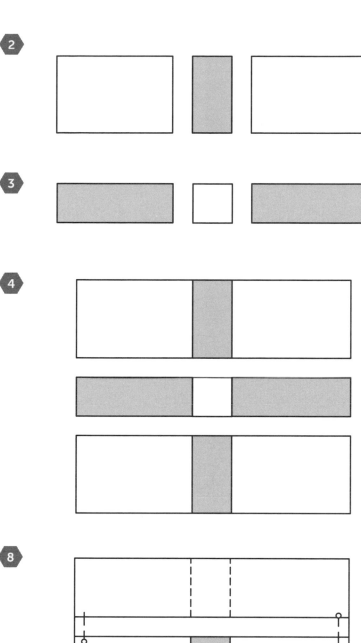

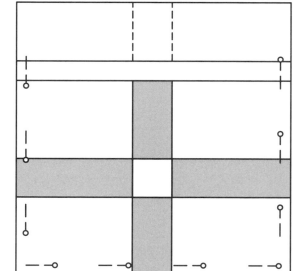

Laid-back Linen

FINISHED SIZE: 19in x 26in

Tea towels are a simple sew, but the result is something that's used daily and always on display in the kitchen. Use a linen fabric, and you create even more organic interest. I added a trim made using a few favourite fabric scraps along the bottom, with hand stitching to give it that homemade feel. The eyelet is a practical detail that also looks good.

Materials:

- 20in x 27in of linen or cotton fabric
- Fabric scraps for trim
- Embroidery thread
- One metal eyelet

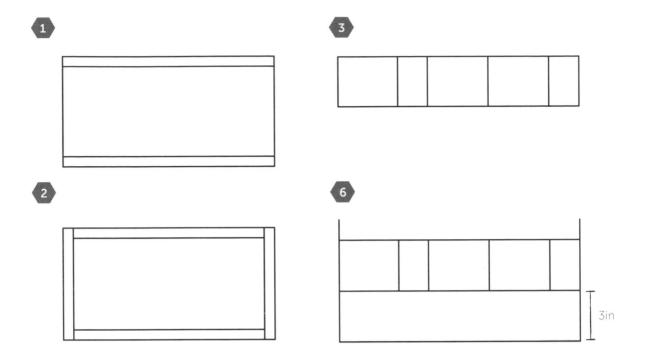

MAKING THE BASIC TEA TOWEL

1 Starting with the long sides of the main fabric, fold the edges inwards ¼in to the wrong side and press. Repeat to hide the raw edge. Sew along both of these edges.

2 Repeat with the short edges.

MAKING THE PIECED BORDER

3 Choose a selection of scrap fabric pieces in various lengths. Cut each one to a width of 3½in. Piece these together along the 3½in edges until you have a row measuring a total of 20in.

4 Starting with the two shorter 3½in wide ends, fold the raw edge inwards ½in to the wrong side and press.

5 Repeat with the longer top and bottom edges.

6 Press this panel and pin in place approximately 3in from the bottom of the tea towel and use embroidery thread to hand stitch close to the edge around all four sides.

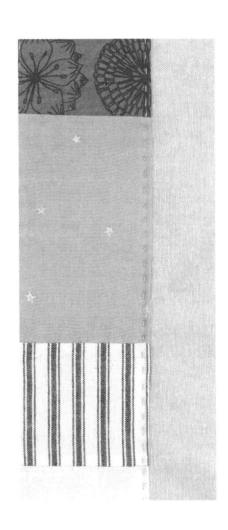

ATTACHING THE HANGER

7 Attach a metal eyelet approximately ½in from one of the top corners of the tea towel. Alternatively, adding the eyelet to the centre of the towel creates a lovely draping effect when hanging up.

Tip

Instead of an eyelet, use a loop of braid for a hanger, sewing this into the top corner in step 2.

Relaxed Dining

FINISHED SIZE: 19in x 76in

Transform your dining space with this informal design. All the detail is at the ends of the runner – rows of simple stitching in the middle will more often than not be covered with your dining bits and bobs. It's a great stash buster with the decorative panels using a mix of fabrics – keep the colour scheme simple and the different fabrics work together just great.

- -

Materials:

- 1yd of main background fabric. If you want to make the runner longer or shorter, simply adjust the length of the centre panel in step 1
- 6in x WOF of striped border fabric
- Twelve assorted 3½in squares for hourglass blocks
- 3in x WOF of hourglass block background fabric
- 1¼yds of backing fabric
- 24in x 84in of wadding (batting)
- Embroidery thread
- ½yd of binding fabric

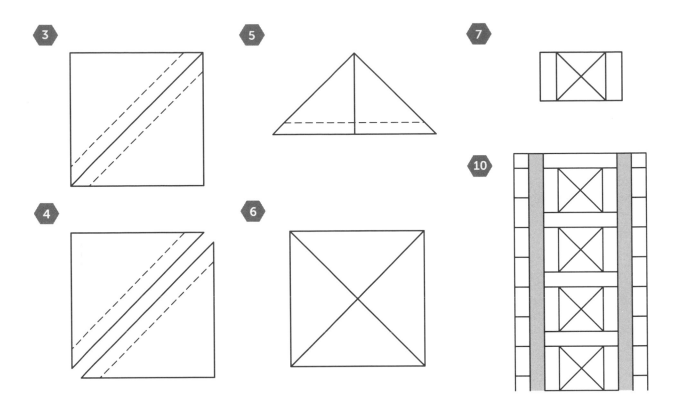

CUTTING

1 Cut out the fabric as follows:

From the main background fabric:

- 19½in x WOF trimmed to 42in for the centre panel
- 9in x WOF strip sub-cut into two 9in x 19½in rectangles for the end panels
- Two 2in x WOF strips sub-cut into four 2in x 19½in strips for the end panel borders

From the striped border fabric:

- Four 1½in x WOF strips sub-cut into four 1½in x 19½in strips for the hourglass panel borders

From the hourglass block background fabric:

- Two 1½in x WOF strips sub-cut into twenty-four 1½in x 2½in rectangles and fourteen 1½in x 4½in rectangles

From the binding fabric:

- Cut five 2½in x WOF strips

TO MAKE THE HOURGLASS BLOCKS

2 Pair up the twelve 3½in squares with right sides facing to create six pairs. With a fabric pencil, draw a diagonal line on the back of the top square. Repeat with all six pairs, then pin each pair together.

3 With a ¼in seam allowance, sew along both sides of the diagonal line.

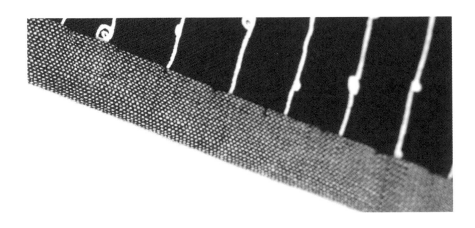

4 With a rotary cutter and ruler, cut along the pencil line. Then turn the ruler around to cut your fabric in the opposite diagonal direction. You now have four separate triangle units.

5 Press these open and then randomly pair together. With right sides facing, matching up the sewn seams, pin in place and sew together with a ¼in seam allowance.

6 Press the block open and trim to 2½in square. Repeat with the remaining triangles to make a total of twelve hourglass blocks.

MAKING THE HOURGLASS PANELS

7 Sew a 1½in x 2½in background strip to two opposite sides of all twelve hourglass blocks and press open.

8 Divide the twelve blocks into two sets of six. Join each set of six blocks, alternating each with a 1½in x 4½in background strip, including one at each end. Repeat to create the second strip of blocks. Press these strips open.

ADDING THE STRIPED BORDERS

9 From the main background fabric, sew a 2in x 19½in strip to each side of both hourglass panels.

10 From the striped fabric, sew a 1½in x 19½in strip on to either side of the above panels.

11 With right sides together, sew the two 19½in x 42in main background panels together along the short edges. This is the centre section of the runner.

12 Again with right sides together, sew an hourglass panel to each short end of the centre section.

13 Press the runner top ready for quilting.

QUILTING AND FINISHING

14 Make a quilt sandwich with the backing fabric right side down, wadding (batting) and your runner top piece on top, right side up (see Techniques: Making a Quilt Sandwich).

15 Quilt using your preferred quilting method. I used embroidery thread to hand quilt mine (see Techniques: Hand Quilting) with straight lines of running stitches to enhance the panels at either end and create little details in the centre panel.

16 Trim the quilt sandwich to 19in x 76in.

17 Bind to finish (see Techniques: Binding Your Quilt).

Randomly Placed

FINISHED SIZE: 12in x 16in

Placemats can add a bit of pizazz to your table with very little effort. Make them all to match, or add snippets of different fabrics for more interest. Incorporating pops of colour with contrasting solid and patterned fabrics can create a really unique look. I left my placemats without any additional detail but you can personalize yours by adding some hand embroidery – it makes a lovely finishing touch, especially if they are a gift.

- -

Materials (to make four placemats):

- ¾yd background fabric
- One fat-quarter of main flying geese fabric
- Two 2⅞in squares of fabric for alternative colour flying geese wing (optional)
- ¾yd backing fabric
- 8in braid for decorative tag (optional)

CUTTING

1 Cut out the fabric as follows:

From the background fabric, cut four sets of the following – one for each placemat:

- Five 2⅞in squares
- Two 2½in squares
- One 2½in x 6½in strip
- Two 1½in x 6½in strips
- One 2½in x 12½in strip
- One 8½in x 12½in rectangle

From the main flying geese fabric:

- Five 5¼in squares

From the backing fabric:

- Four 12½in x 16½in rectangles

From the braid, if using:

- Four 2in pieces

PLACEMAT FRONT

2 Using the Four-At-a-Time Flying Geese method, make five sets of four flying geese from the 5¼in main fabric squares and the 2⅞in squares of background fabric (see Techniques: Flying Geese). If you are incorporating a random coloured wing into each placemat, make sure you use your two alternative colour squares as above.

3 Press the wings' seams outwards and use five flying geese for each placemat.

4 To construct the flying geese column, sew together three flying geese and press. Then sew the 2½in x 6½in strip on the right-hand side. Next sew and press one 2½in square onto the left-hand side of one flying geese unit and one on the right-hand side of the last remaining flying geese unit. Sew these two underneath your column of three flying geese and press.

5 Sew and press one 1½in x 6½in strip to the top of this piece and one to the bottom. Your piece should now measure 6½in x 12½in.

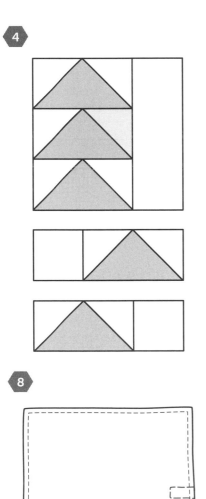

6 Finally sew and press the 2½in x 12½in strip on the left-hand side and the 8½in x 12½in piece on the right-hand side.

7 Repeat for the remaining three placemat fronts.

MAKING UP

8 With right sides facing, pin the front and back pieces together. If you are adding the decorative tag, fold a 2in length of braid in half and position in between the front and back layers with the folded edge of the tag inside.

9 Sew around the four sides leaving a 5in gap for turning.

10 Snip across each corner to give crisper corners to your placemat and then turn right sides out.

11 Press the placemat, folding the unsewn section of fabric inwards. Sew around the edge of the placemat to close up the gap and create a neat finish. Stitch a second line approximately ¾in inside the first to create a defined border.

12 Repeat for the remaining three placemats.

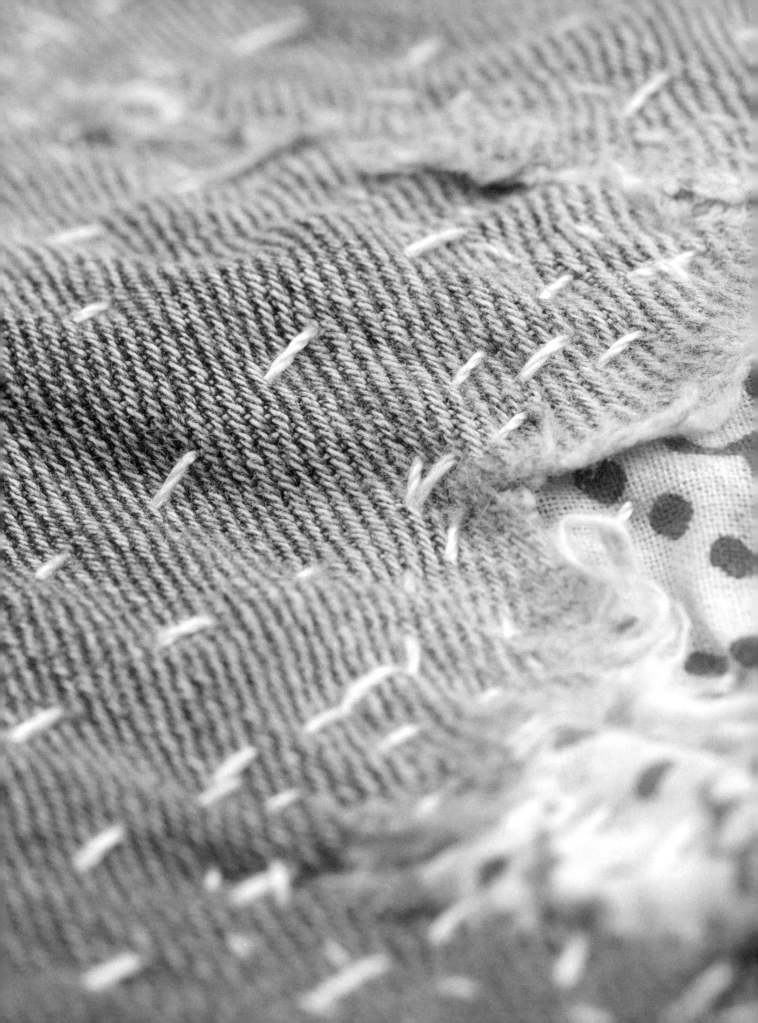

EXPLORING

Venturing out and about nourishes
our soul with inspiration and energy,
so keep the spirit of wabi-sabi on
you at all times in your clothes and
accessories. Make, mend and marvel at
the organic beauty of your belongings
while enjoying our big wide world.

Indigo Anywhere

FINISHED SIZE: 6½in x 8½in

With its off-centre design, hand quilting and indigo dyed fabric, this pouch oozes wabi-sabi vibes. You can make it more so by using all those tiny scraps of fabric you have for each different piece. The pouch is a perfect size to keep all sorts of things safe such as an on-the-go EPP project, expense receipts or even as a passport travel pouch. Just throw it in your bag and you're ready to go.

Materials

- One fat-quarter of dark indigo fabric
- One 7in square of light indigo fabric
- One fat-eighth of lining fabric
- 8in x 13in of wadding (batting)
- 12in zipper
- 6in of decorative leather tie (optional)
- 2in of ribbon for decorative tag (optional)
- Embroidery thread

CUTTING

1 Cut out the fabric as follows:

From the dark indigo fabric:
- Three 3in squares
- Four 1½in squares
- One 1½in x 5½in strip
- Two 1½in x 6½in strips
- One 3in x 7in rectangle
- One 7in x 9in rectangle for the back

From the light indigo fabric:
- Three 3in squares
- One 3½in square

From the lining fabric:
- Two 7in x 9in rectangles

MAKING THE CENTRE DESIGN

2 Make three sets of Four-At-a-Time HSTs (see Techniques: Half Square Triangles), yielding a total of twelve HST units.

3 Press each unit open and trim to 1½in square.

4 Sew four rows of three HST units, paying attention to the direction of the light and dark triangles.

5 Sew a strip on either side of the 3½in light indigo square, again paying attention to the direction of the triangles.

6 Sew a 1½in dark indigo square on each end of the two remaining strips, then sew one of these on top of the unit and one on the bottom.

MAKING THE FRONT OF THE POUCH

7 Sew the 1½in x 5½in strip of dark indigo fabric on the right-hand side of the centre block.

8 Sew one 1½in x 6½in strip on top of this unit and one on the bottom.

9 Finally sew the 3in x 7in rectangle on the left-hand side of the unit.

10 Sew the pouch back to the bottom of this unit.

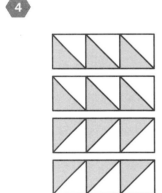

4

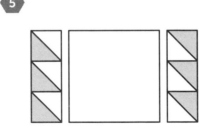

5

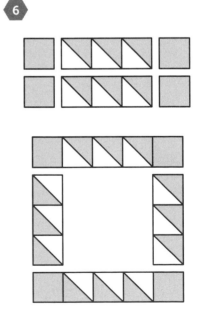

6

QUILTING THE POUCH OUTER

11 Spray baste the wadding (batting) on the back of the unit you have just made and quilt as desired (see Techniques: Hand Quilting). I used embroidery thread to hand stitch straight lines across the front and back. By folding the purse in half and marking points on the front and back you can make sure the stitched lines meet.

ATTACHING THE ZIPPER

12 With the zipper fully open and with right sides facing, pin one edge of the zipper to the front of the purse outer, aligning the opening end of the zipper with the edge of the purse outer.

13 With the zipper foot on your machine, sew along this edge, resting the foot edge against the zipper teeth.

14 With right sides together, position one of the lining pieces on top of the zipper, pin in place and sew, sandwiching the zipper between the pouch outer and lining.

15 Repeat with the other side of the pouch and zipper.

16 Partially close the zipper, bringing the zipper pull inside the pouch. Leave the zipper partially open for turning.

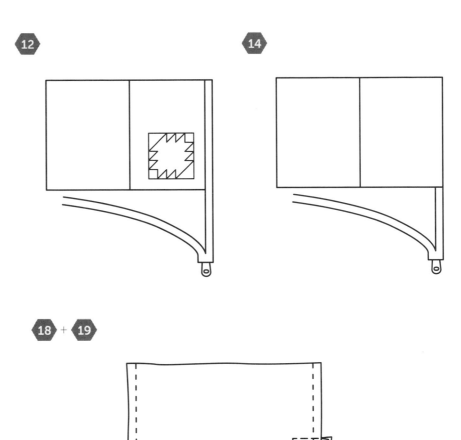

MAKING THE POUCH

17 Open out the pouch so that the right sides of the pouch outer are together and the right sides of the lining are together. The zipper should be in the middle, facing the lining. Pin in place.

18 If you are adding the decorative ribbon tag, fold this in half, place the folded edge inwards and align the cut edges with the edge of the pouch outer near to the zipper end. Pin in place.

19 Stitch across the two sides of the pouch, sewing carefully across the zipper as you go. Do not sew across the bottom of the lining as you will be turning the pouch through this gap.

20 Push the pouch through the zipper and lining gap. Push out the corners of the pouch outer and leave the lining outside the pouch.

21 Press the lining gap seam inwards and sew shut as close to the fold as you can. Push the lining into the pouch.

22 If using, tie the leather to the zipper pull.

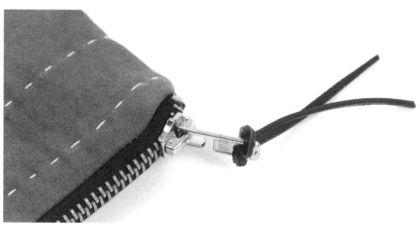

Carried Along

FINISHED SIZE: 13in x 15in

I can never have too many bags. Whether I'm popping to the shops, travelling away from home with a sewing project, or strolling the streets of an exciting new place, I want a tote to hold all of my essentials with room for more. This bag is perfect for just those and many more occasions. The strap works on the shoulder, but is also long enough to wear across your body.

Materials:

- ½yd denim weight fabric for the outer
- Ten 3in x 5in scraps of quilting weight cotton for the hexagons
- 2in x 12in quilting weight cotton for the squares
- ½yd quilting weight cotton for the lining
- ¾in x 36in leather strap
- Leather hole punch
- Four brass rivets

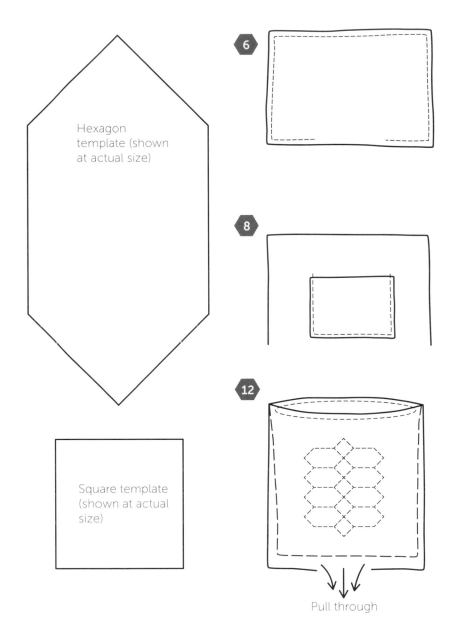

Hexagon template (shown at actual size)

Square template (shown at actual size)

Pull through

CUTTING

1 Cut out the fabric as follows:

From the denim weight fabric:

- Two 13½in x 15½in rectangles

From the lining fabric:

- Two 13½in x 15½in rectangles
- One 9in x 12in rectangle

TOTE FRONT

2 Use the two templates to make ten elongated hexagons and six squares with EPP (see Techniques: English Paper Piecing). Press all of the pieces and then carefully remove the papers. Press again if any lose their shape.

3 Arrange the pieces on the front of the tote until you are happy with the layout and then pin in place.

4 Machine or hand sew the pieces onto the tote. Sew each piece as close to the fold lines as you can to keep them flat.

MAKING UP

5 With right sides of the tote outer pieces facing, pin and sew around the two sides and base. Snip across the corners to avoid bulk and then turn right sides out.

MAKING THE LINING POCKET

6 Fold the 9in x 12in lining pocket fabric in half, with right sides facing, to create a 9in x 6in rectangle. Pin in place and sew around the edges, leaving a 4in gap for turning in one of the longer sides.

7 Trim the corners, turn right sides out and press firmly.

ATTACHING THE POCKET TO THE LINING

8 Pin the pocket onto the right side of one of the lining pieces, 4in from the top, positioning the unsewn gap of the pocket at the base.

9 Sew around the two sides and the base of the pocket to attach it to the lining, sewing a couple of extra forward-and-backward stitches at the top to add strength.

MAKING AND ATTACHING THE LINING

10 Make the lining in the same way as the tote outer but leaving a 6in gap at the bottom for turning.

11 With right sides facing, put the tote outer inside the lining, taking care to align the seams. Ensure the back of the lining and outer are together. Pin together the raw edges of the outer and lining, and sew all the way around.

12 Pull the tote outer through the lining gap. When you have turned the lining right sides out, press the lining gap seam inwards and sew across as close to the fold as you can. Push the lining into the bag and press the lining and tote outer seam flat.

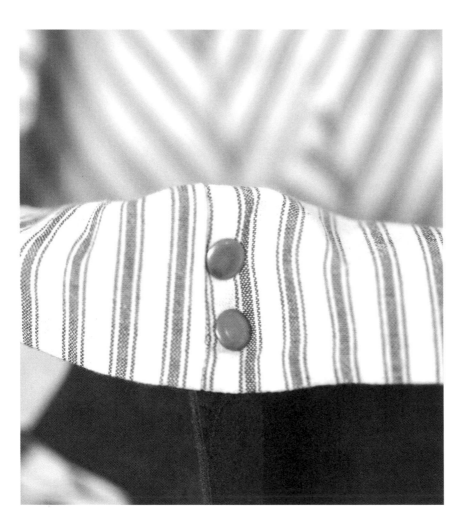

ATTACHING THE STRAP

13 Punch two holes at either side of the tote with the leather hole punch: the first should be ¾in from the top of the tote and the second should be a further ¾in down.

14 Punch two holes at either end of the leather strap: the first should be ½in from the end of the strap and the second should be a further ¾in up.

15 Align the holes and attach a metal rivet through each hole, following the manufacturer's instructions, to secure the strap in place.

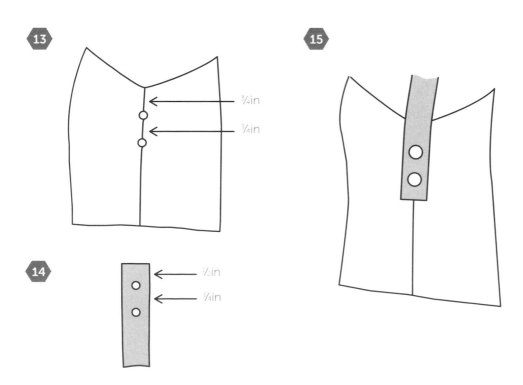

13

¾in

¾in

14

½in

¾in

15

Informal Mixer

FINISHED SIZE: 17in x 99in

A scarf is a great afternoon project – just raid your stash and sew. I patchworked the front, and backed it with a soft jersey, but you could piece both sides. The fabric patterns create harmonious effect as I included my favourite blooms and checks, then matched them with a textured woven solid. The resulting palette is simple, but you may prefer something more lively. So pull out your fabrics and have fun creating!

- -

Materials:

- Variety of fabrics at least 18in wide each for the front. The total length should add up to 100in plus an additional ½in for each fabric chosen to allow for seam allowances
- 1½yds backing fabric
- Embroidery thread

CUTTING

1 Cut out the fabric as follows:

From the fabric for the front:
- Cut 18in widths

From the backing fabric:
- Three 18in x WOF rectangles

MAKING THE SCARF FRONT

2 Lay out your fabrics and put them into your chosen arrangement.

3 With right sides facing, pin and sew each piece together.

4 Press your scarf front and trim to 100in.

MAKING THE SCARF BACK

5 Sew the three lengths of backing fabric together, press and trim to the same length as your scarf front.

MAKING UP THE SCARF

6 With right sides facing, pin the scarf front and back together.

7 Sew around the four sides, leaving a 10in gap in one of the long edges for turning.

8 Snip across each corner to reduce bulk when turned. Be careful not to cut the stitching.

9 Turn your scarf the right way out and press all around. Press the edges of the unsewn gap inwards and pin the two edges together.

10 Hand sew an $\frac{1}{8}$in running stitch along both long edges using embroidery thread. This not only sews up the gap, but also adds a lovely decorative touch.

Well Worn

FINISHED SIZE: Customizable

My jeans are always getting worn at the knees – I think it's all the crawling around on the floor basting quilts! Breathing extra life into much loved clothing is such a joy and a relief, and making a feature of the love of a much used item gives it added character. This is a great activity to slowly stitch life back into favourite pieces. The techniques shown here are perfect for mending other items.

Materials:

TO MEND THE HOLES
- Cotton fabric
- Strong card
- Embroidery thread

TO MEND THE HEM
- 2½in wide strip of binding fabric

CUTTING

1 Cut out the materials as follows:

Patching a hole

- Cut a patch of fabric on the bias to allow stretch and ease of movement. This patch needs to be the width of your jeans leg, just inside from seam to seam, and at least 2in larger than the height of the hole

- Cut the card the width of the jeans leg and at least 4in larger than the height of the hole

For the hem

- Cut the fabric 3in x circumference of the leg hem, plus 4in

SEWING THE KNEE PATCH

2 Position the card inside the jeans leg, behind the hole. This helps to separate the front and back of the leg, making it easier to pin the patch in place.

3 Feed the patch through the hole and smooth it out underneath. Pin in place all around the hole and the edges of the patch itself.

4 With a fabric pencil, draw lines approximately ¼in apart across the area you are sewing, from seam to seam of the jeans.

5 Starting in the centre of the patch, sew a row of running stitches from side to side. Do this by pulling the knotted thread through from the inside.

6 Sew each new row on the opposite side of the previous row, smoothing out the fabric patch as you go. Always finish off a thread with a knot on the inside.

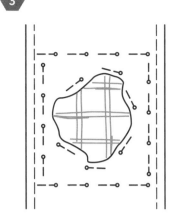

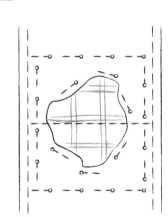

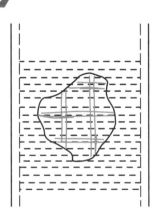

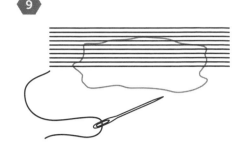

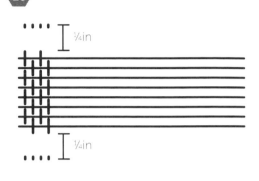

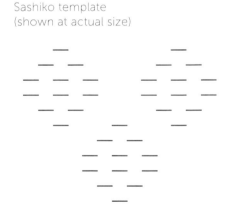

Sashiko template
(shown at actual size)

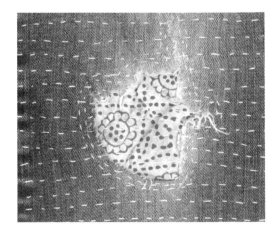

7 Continue until you have sewn across the whole hole, then keep sewing more rows above and below to secure the patch in place.

8 You can highlight the hole by sewing a couple of rows around the edge of it, echoing the shape. This has the added benefit of further securing the patch. I also added a few rows of sashiko-style crosses above the patch for added detail.

DARNING THE HOLE

9 With the card inside the leg for stabilizing, stitch horizontal lines close together across the rip, starting ½in away from the rip and moving from top to bottom. Secure the thread with a knot inside the leg at the end.

10 For the vertical lines, keep the embroidery thread the same colour, or change it to add interest. Starting from the left or right edge, weave the thread in and out of your horizontal lines. When you have completed the first vertical row, sew a small stitch approximately ¼in away to make your darning extra secure. Push each new row close to the previous one to create a dense weave.

11 Keep going until you have darned across the whole area; don't forget to make a small stitch ¼in away at the end of every vertical row.

ADDING THE SASHIKO

12 To enhance the darn, I stitched several decorative sashiko shapes around it – three above and two below. Decide where you want to stitch yours and transfer the template onto the right side.

13 Starting with the top horizontal line, stitch horizontally across this through the fabric. Continue onto the next row when you reach the end, re-threading your needle as required.

14 When you have finished all the horizontal stitches, tie off your thread at the back.

15 Working from one side to the other, stitch the vertical lines to complete the sashiko pattern. The pattern will be revealed as you go

MENDING THE HEM

16 Press your binding fabric strip, wrong sides together, in half lengthways.

17 Bind the hem as you would a raw edge (see Techniques: Binding a Raw Edge).

Irregular Beauty

FINISHED SIZE: 50in x 50in

Courthouse Steps is the perfect design for a picnic quilt – one giant block with 'steps' radiating from the centre. Traditionally the same colour is used on opposite sections as I've done, but I snuck in a splash of contrasting red, joining different fabrics to make the required length strips. This is a useful technique if you have to join strips of the same colour or print to obtain wide enough steps. Different fabrics add interest, so don't worry about matching!

Materials:

- 1½yds in total of Colour 1 fabric (low volume)
- 1½yds in total of Colour 2 fabric (blue)
- 2½in x WOF strip of contrast fabric (red) (optional)
- 4yds of backing fabric
- 60in square of wadding (batting)
- ½yd of binding fabric

CUTTING

1 Using the cutting plan, cut out the fabric as follows:

From Colour 1 fabric cut fifteen 2½in x WOF strips, then:

- From four strips cut four 40½in strips
- From two strips cut two 38½in strips and two 2½in squares
- From two strips cut two 34½in strips and two 6½in strips
- From two strips cut two 30½in strips and two 10½in strips
- From two strips cut two 26½in strips and two 14½in strips
- From two strips cut two 22½in strips and two 18½in strips
- From one strip cut one 6½in strip and two 2½in squares

From Colour 2 fabric cut seventeen 2½in x WOF strips, then:

- From six strips cut six 40½in strips
- From two strips cut two 38½in strips and one 2½in square
- From two strips cut two 34½in strips and two 6½in strips
- From two strips cut two 30½in strips and two 10½in strips
- From two strips cut two 26½in strips and two 14½in strips
- From two strips cut two 22½in strips and two 18½in strips
- From one strip cut two 10½in strips, two 6½in strips and two 2½in squares

From the backing fabric cut:

- Two pieces 2yds x 30in

From the binding fabric cut:

- Six strips 2½in x WOF

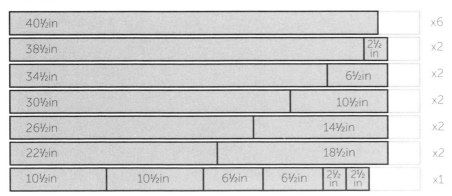

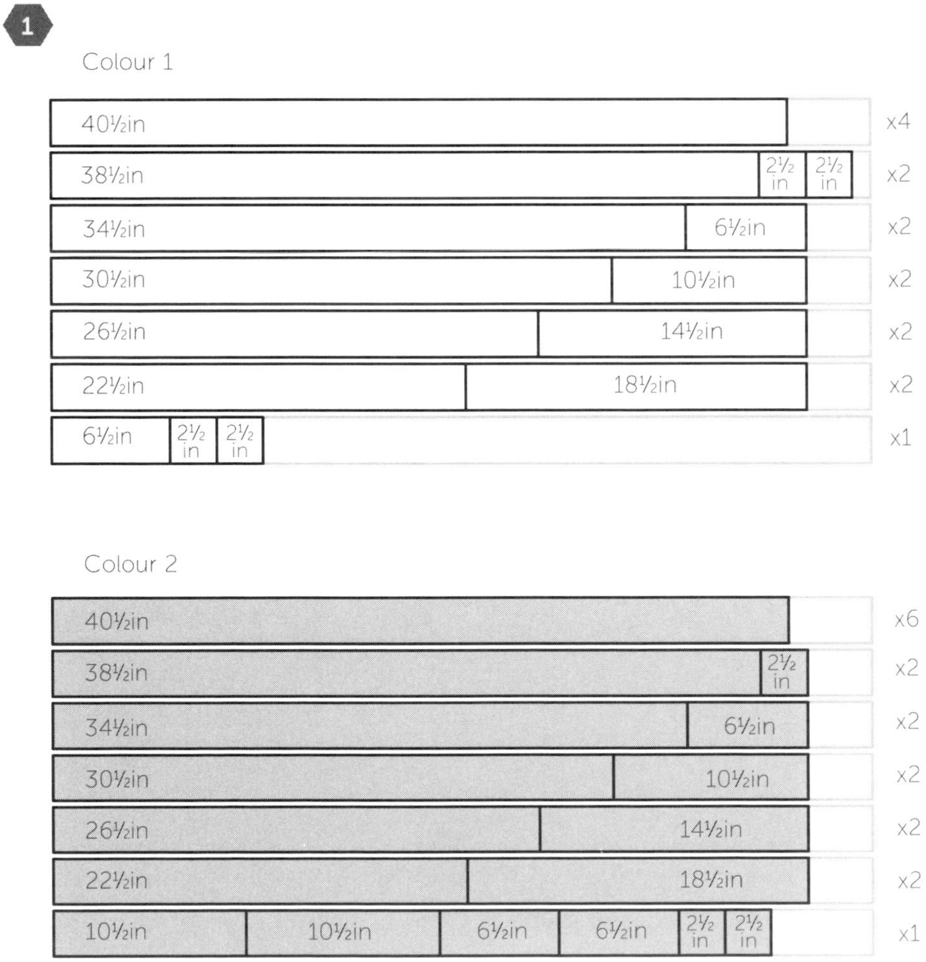

1

Colour 1

40½in	x4
38½in · 2½in · 2½in	x2
34½in · 6½in	x2
30½in · 10½in	x2
26½in · 14½in	x2
22½in · 18½in	x2
6½in · 2½in · 2½in	x1

Colour 2

40½in	x6
38½in · 2½in	x2
34½in · 6½in	x2
30½in · 10½in	x2
26½in · 14½in	x2
22½in · 18½in	x2
10½in · 10½in · 6½in · 6½in · 2½in · 2½in	x1

Total yield

Colour 1:
Four 40½in strips
Two 38½in strips
Two 34½in strips
Two 30½in strips
Two 26½in strips
Two 22½in strips
Two 18½in strips
Two 14½in strips
Two 10½in strips
Three 6½in strips
Six 2½in squares

Colour 2:
Six 40½in strips
Two 38½in strips
Two 34½in strips
Two 30½in strips
Two 26½in strips
Two 22½in strips
Two 18½in strips
Two 14½in strips
Four 10½in strips
Four 6½in strips
Four 2½in squares

PREPARING THE STRIPS

2 To create the longer strips from those you have just cut, join the following with a ¼in seam allowance:

From Colour 1, join:

- One 40½in strip and one 2½in square. Repeat with another 40½in strip and 2½in square
- One 40½in strip and one 6½in strip. Repeat with another 40½in strip and 6½in strip

From Colour 2, join:

- One 40½in strip and one 2½in square. Repeat with another 40½in strip and 2½in square
- One 40½in strip and one 6½in strip. Repeat with another 40½in strip and 6½in strip
- One 40½in strip and one 10½in strip. Repeat with another 40½in strip and 10½in strip

MAKING THE QUILT TOP

3 Take one 2½in Colour 2 square (this will be the centre square) and one 2½in Colour 1 square. With right sides facing, pin and sew along one side. Take the second 2½in Colour 1 square and repeat on the opposite side of the centre square. Press the seams outwards.

4 Take the 6½in Colour 2 strip and sew on either side of this unit, then press.

5 Continue alternating and adding each subsequent pair of strips in this fashion until you have added the final 50½in Colour 2 strips. Piecing these long strips can sometimes be tricky; if the long outer edges look as if they are bowing, trim to straighten.

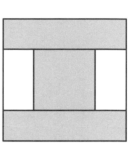

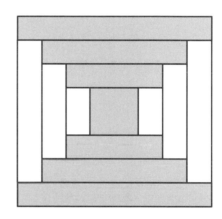

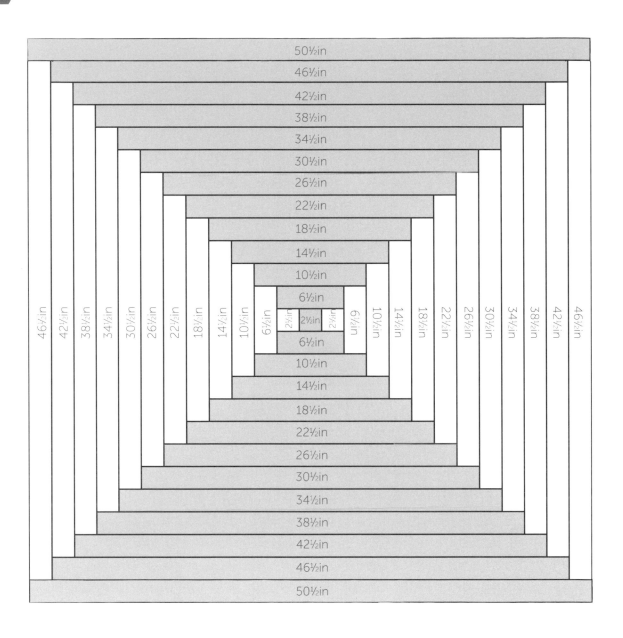

6 Use the layout diagram to help you keep track of the strips as you add each one.

QUILTING AND FINISHING

7 Sew the two pieces of backing fabric together along the long sides with a ½in seam allowance. Press the seam open.

8 Make a quilt sandwich with the backing fabric right side down, wadding (batting) and your pieced top right side up (see Techniques: Making a Quilt Sandwich).

9 Quilt with your preferred method. I machine quilted around each row, deciding that machine quilting would be harder wearing for a well-used picnic blanket.

10 Trim the quilt sandwich to 50in x 50in.

11 To finish, bind the quilt, taking care to mitre the corners neatly (see Techniques: Binding Your Quilt).

SLEEPING

Rest recharges our creativity, and retreating to a peaceful haven in your home allows this. From organizing your wardrobe to adding the comforting informality of wabi-sabi to your bedding, you're halfway to dreamland before your head even hits the pillow.

Creating Calm

FINISHED SIZE: 17in x 18in

I like a place for everything and everything in its place. It makes me feel organized even if I'm not! When travelling, I have bags for underwear, socks, tights and so on, with each distinguishable so that I can grab what I need quickly. With graphic 'plus' blocks in a solid colour, this one is just that. The teeny 1½in squares may look fiddly, but they're sewn in strips for minimal effort and perfect for scraps you saved for who knows when.

- -

Materials:

- One fat-quarter of solid fabric for 'plus' blocks
- ¾yd in total of background fabric
- ½yd of lining fabric
- 6in x 18in of fabric for ribbon casing
- 50in of ribbon
- ½yd of wadding (batting)
- Embroidery thread for hand quilting (optional)

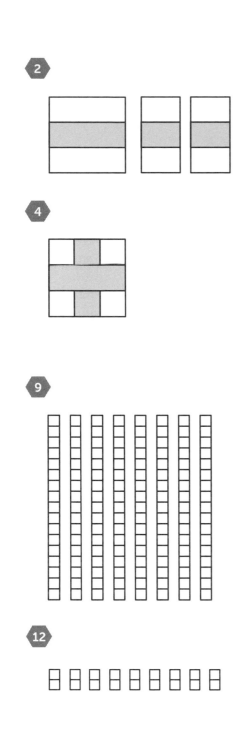

CUTTING

1 Cut out the fabric as follows:

From the solid fabric:

- Eighteen 1½in x 3in rectangles
- Eighteen 1½in x 3½in rectangles

From the background fabric:

- Thirty-six 1½in x 3in rectangles
- Thirty-four 1½in x 12in strips
- Sixteen 1½in x 13½in strips

From the lining:

- Two 17½in x 17½in squares

From the ribbon casing:

- Two 3in x 18in strips

From the wadding (batting):

- Two 18in x 22in rectangles

MAKING THE 'PLUS' BLOCKS

2 Take one 1½in x 3in rectangle of solid fabric and sew one 1½in x 3in rectangle of background fabric to both sides, along the long edges. Press and cut in half to create two identical 1½in x 3½in units.

3 Repeat with the remaining seventeen sets. You need nine sets for the front and nine for the back so randomly pair them up.

4 Take two random pieced units from above and press. Sew one along each long side of a 1½in x 3½in rectangle of solid fabric. You should have one 'plus' block.

5 Repeat with the remaining pieces to create a total of eighteen 'plus' blocks.

6 Choose nine 'plus' blocks for the front, and nine for the back, and set aside for later.

Tip

Make your bag even more wabi-sabi by using a variety of different fabrics for the 'pluses'.

MAKING THE LONG BACKGROUND ROWS

7 Randomly arrange the thirty-four 1½in x 12in background strips into two sets of seventeen and sew each set together.

8 Press these carefully but don't worry if they pull out of shape a little – this is wabi-sabi after all.

9 Cut across each of these sets at 1½in intervals. Each set should yield eight strips.

10 Pick two strips at random, sew together along their length and press. Repeat with the remaining strips, making eight sets – four background rows for the front and four for the back.

MAKING THE BACKGROUND BETWEEN THE 'PLUS' BLOCKS

11 Randomly arrange the thirty-six 1½in x 3in background rectangles into eight pairs and sew each pair together along the long sides. Press carefully.

12 Cut each pair into nine 1½in x 3½in rectangles.

13 Randomly take three pairs, sew together along the long sides and press.

14 Repeat with the remaining pieces to make twenty-four units of two-by-three.

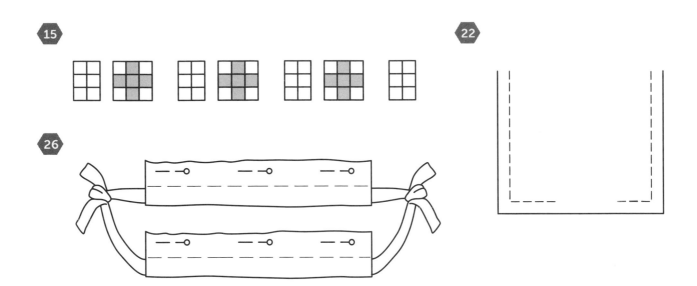

MAKING UP THE FRONT AND BACK

15 Take four of the two-by-three units and three 'plus' blocks and sew together alternately.

16 Repeat with the remaining units to make a total of six 'plus' rows, then press.

17 Take four background rows and three 'plus' rows and sew together alternately. This will be the front of your bag.

18 Repeat with the remaining units to make the back.

19 Press your front and back pieces ready to quilt.

QUILTING AND MAKING UP THE OUTER BAG

20 Tack (baste) the front and the back onto the wadding (batting) pieces and quilt as desired. I used embroidery thread to hand quilt rows of running-stitch along the diagonal to break up the regular patchwork. Trim both the front and back pieces to 18in x 22in.

21 With right sides together, pin the quilted front and back of the bag together. Sew around the two long sides and bottom of the front and back of the cover. Turn this the right way round, pushing the corners out for a crisp finish.

MAKING THE LINING

22 With right sides together, pin the lining pieces. Sew around the two long sides and bottom of the of the lining. Leave a 5in gap along the bottom for turning and leave the lining inside out for now.

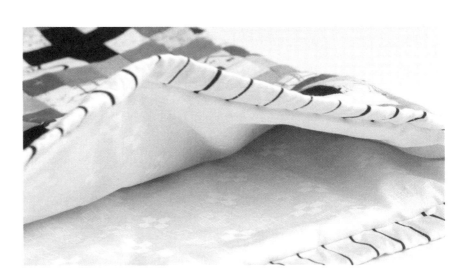

MAKING THE RIBBON CASING

23 Take one of the 3in x 18in strips, fold the short ends in by 1in to the wrong side and sew in place. Repeat with the other strip.

24 Fold both strips in half lengthways, wrong sides together, and press.

25 Tie a knot in the ends of the ribbon to create a large loop.

26 With raw edges aligned and right sides facing, pin one casing to the front and one on the back of the bag. As you are pinning, push the ribbon down against the fold of the casing, to avoid the pins.

27 Sew all the way round the casing, making sure the ribbon is still pushed down to the folded side of the casing so that it doesn't get sewn in.

MAKING UP THE BAG

28 Keeping the casing and ribbon facing downwards, push the bag outer inside the lining so that the right sides of the inner and outer are facing. The casing should be hidden between the two.

29 Pin around the top, lining up the seams and sew around with a ⅜in seam allowance to hide the casing stitches and give a neat finish.

30 Pull the bag outer through the gap in the lining. Once fully through, fold the raw edges of the lining gap inwards and stitch the gap closed by hand or machine.

31 Push the lining down into the bag so that the corners meet and smooth into place.

Hanging Out

FINISHED SIZE: 8½in x 17in

Fed up with your spare hangers clanging around and getting tangled in the wardrobe? These little covers are the answer – quick and easy to sew, they also look fabulous. Don't worry if you don't have large enough pieces of fabric, as you can make them from a single piece, or sew 18in wide strips together. I've done this in a couple of cases and love the patchwork effect, plus it's a great way to use up odds and ends in your stash.

- -

Materials (for one cover):

- One fat-quarter of fabric
- Coat hanger of your choice

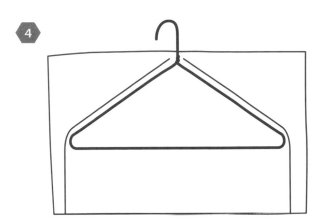

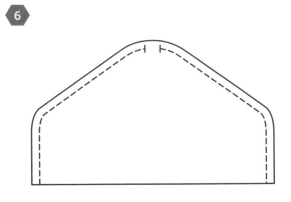

CUTTING

1 Cut out the fabric as follows:

- Two 11in x 18in rectangles, either from one piece of fabric, or from a patchwork of smaller pieces

MAKING UP THE HANGER

2 Fold the bottom hem of both pieces of fabric under by ¼in and press. Repeat to hide the raw edge, then sew along both hems.

3 Fold one of the rectangles, wrong sides together, in half along the 18in side. Gently press the halfway point to mark it. Position the base of the hanger's neck ½in down from this mark on the wrong side.

4 With a fabric pencil draw down the sloping shoulders of the hanger, leaving a ¼in gap between the hanger and the pencil line – this will accommodate the seam. When you reach the end, continue the line straight down to the bottom edge of the fabric.

5 With right sides facing, pin the two rectangles of fabric together, and with a rotary cutter trim away the excess fabric following the pencil line.

6 Sew ¼in away from the drawn line, leaving a ¼in gap at the centre top for the hook. Reverse stitch a few times at this point to strengthen the opening. You can trim the raw edges with pinking shears or sew with a zigzag stitch to prevent fraying, but if you aren't frequently removing the cover it won't get much wear.

7 Turn the cover the right way out, smooth the seams and press flat.

Simple Stitches

FINISHED SIZE: 19in x 30in

I am a big fan of plain, crisp white bed linen – white sheets and a white duvet cover. But to break that up, I like to have pillowcases that add an extra bit of detail. These easy-to-sew pillowcases, with a variety of hand stitching, are the perfect addition to a simple bedroom scheme. Choose one of the stitch designs to retain the simplicity, or jazz it up by including more than one.

Materials (for one pillowcase):

- 1¼yds of fabric
- Embroidery thread

CUTTING

1 Cut out the fabric as follows:

- One 20½in x 32in rectangle for the front
- One 20½in x 40in rectangle for the back

HEMMING THE FRONT AND BACK

2 With the smaller (front) rectangle, fold one of the shorter edges inwards ¼in to the wrong side and press. Repeat to hide the raw edge then sew along this edge.

3 Repeat with the larger (back) piece.

HAND STITCHING THE CIRCLES

4 Fold the pillowcase front in half lengthways and press lightly. This will be your guide line for stitching.

5 Make a template of the circle (see Templates), then cut it out.

6 Fold the circle template in half and half again to find the centre. Snip away this point to allow you to view the centre line on the fabric and line up the template perfectly.

7 Position the circle on the centre line, 2½in from the hemmed side. Draw round with a fabric pencil. Draw a row of five circles all touching and 2½in from the hemmed side. Then draw a second row, identical to, and touching, the first row.

8 Draw vertical lines through the circle centre and then horizontal lines through each pair.

9 Using your embroidery thread, hand sew a running stitch around all ten circles and through all the lines.

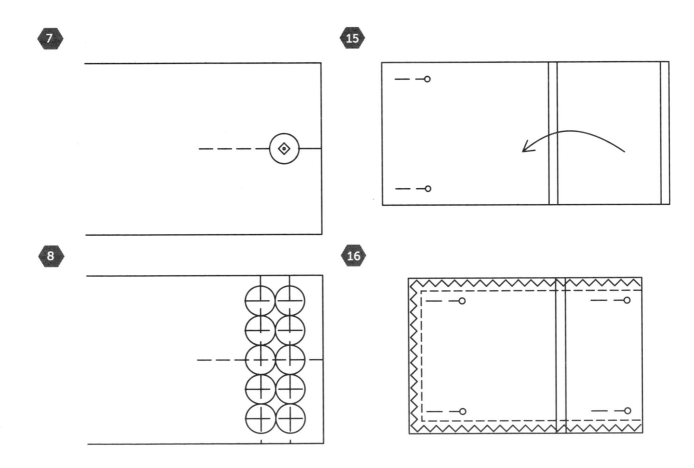

HAND STITCHING THE SASHIKO

10 Prepare the pillowcase front as step 4. Copy the sashiko template (see Templates) and transfer three times onto the right side of the fabric. Centre the first motif using the folded line. Leave a gap of approximately 2in between each motif and 4in from the edge of the fabric.

11 Start by stitching across the top horizontal line. Continue onto the next horizontal row and each subsequent one, re-threading your needle as required. Use one stitch to span the shorter lines, and two for the longer lines.

12 When you have finished the horizontal stitches, tie off your thread at the back.

13 Working from one side to the other, refer to the photograph and stitch the vertical lines to complete the pattern.

MAKING UP THE PILLOWCASE

14 With right sides together, match the shorter raw edges, and pin the three raw edges together.

15 Fold the hemmed excess fabric of the back piece over the wrong side of the front piece and pin.

16 Sew around the three open sides leaving a ¼in seam allowance. For extra strength, sew a row of zigzag stitch along the three raw edges.

17 Turn the pillowcase the right way out and pop a pillow inside.

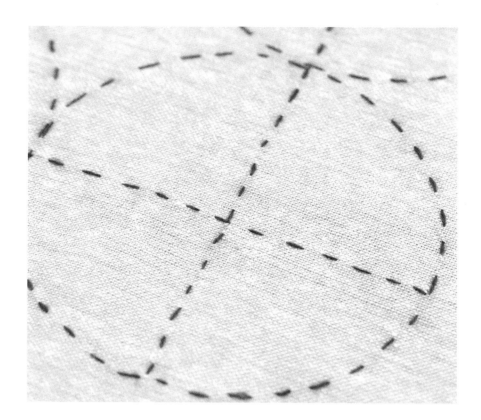

Heirloom Hugs

FINISHED SIZE: 9½in x 15½in*

There's nothing like cosying up with a hot water bottle, and if it's encased in an equally cosy handmade cover, even better. I made this one out of soft hand dyed fabric that gives a lovely homely feel. The delicately pieced design and hand quilting gives the effect of a long-standing family heirloom. A tie fastening makes it easy to pop out your bottle for quick and easy heating.

- -

Materials:

- ½yd of main fabric
- One fat-sixteenth of secondary fabric for design
- One fat-quarter of lining fabric
- 18in x 22in of wadding (batting)
- Embroidery thread for hand quilting (optional)
- 26in of ribbon

NB *The measurements and materials given are for an 8in x 14in hot water bottle, the result being a cover 1½in wider and taller than the bottle. If your bottle is a different size, add 3in to the dimensions of your bottle to get the size of the front and back cover and lining pieces. For example, if your hot water bottle measures 7in x 12in, these pieces should be cut to 10in x 15in. As you make up the cover front, the borders you add will vary, but you can sew as per the instructions and trim at the end as needed.*

CUTTING

1 Cut out the fabric as follows:

From the main fabric cut:

- One 10in x 16in rectangle for the back
- Two 1½in x 3in rectangles (a)
- Two 1in x 3½in rectangles (b)
- Two 1in x 4½in rectangles (c)
- Eight 1½in x 2½in rectangles (d)
- Four 1½in squares (e)
- Four 1½in x 3½in rectangles (f)
- One 5in square (HSTs)
- Twelve 1⅞in squares (flying geese)

- One 2½in x 8½in rectangle (g)
- One 4in x 8½in rectangle (h)
- Two 1in x 16in strips (i)

From the secondary fabric cut:

- One 1½in x 3½in rectangle (j)
- One 1½in x 3in rectangle (k)
- One 5in square (HSTs)
- Three 3¼in squares (flying geese)

From the lining fabric:

- Two 11in x 18in rectangles

From the wadding (batting):

- Two 11in x 18in rectangles

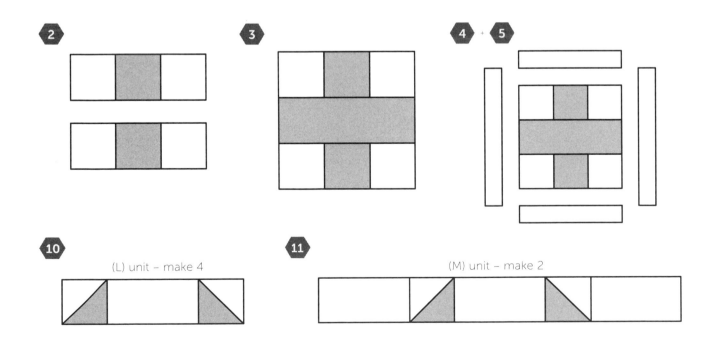

(L) unit – make 4

(M) unit – make 2

MAKING THE CENTRAL 'PLUS' BLOCK

2 Position piece (k) in the middle of both (a) pieces and sew together. Press and cut in half to give two 1½in x 3½in pieces.

3 Position piece (j) in the middle of both of the above pieces, sew together and then press.

4 Take both (b) pieces and sew one on the left of the above block and one on the right, then press.

5 Take both (c) pieces and sew one on the top of the above block and one on the bottom, then press.

MAKING THE HSTs

6 From the main and secondary fabric 5in squares, make one set of eight HSTs using the Eight-At-a-Time HST method (see Techniques: Half Square Triangles). This will yield eight HSTs.

7 Trim to 1½in square.

MAKING THE FLYING GEESE

8 From the twelve main fabric 1⅞in squares and three secondary fabric 3¼in squares, make three sets of flying geese using the Four-At-a-Time Flying Geese method (see Techniques: Flying Geese). This will yield 12 flying geese units.

9 Trim to 1½in x 2½in.

PIECING THE FRONT

10 Sew a (d) piece between two HSTs, making sure the secondary fabric square is bottom down and facing inwards, as below. Press this and repeat with all four sets to make four (L) units.

11 Take two of these (L) units and sew a (d) piece on either end, to create two (M) units.

12

(N) unit – make 2

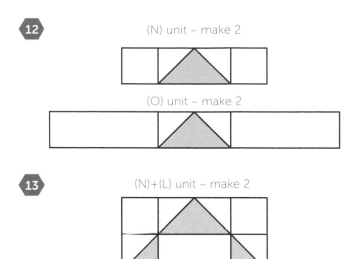

(O) unit – make 2

13

(N)+(L) unit – make 2

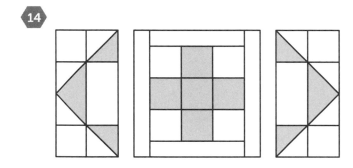

14

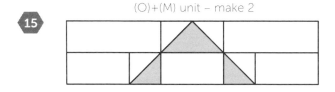

(O)+(M) unit – make 2

15

16

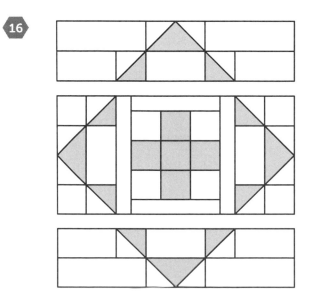

12 Take two of the flying geese and sew an (f) piece on either end to make two (N) units. Take two further flying geese and sew an (e) piece on either end to make two (O) units. Press all these units.

13 To make the unit on the left side of the central 'plus' block, sew together units (N) and (L) making sure they are facing in the correct direction. Repeat to make the opposite side.

14 Press these units, then sew onto opposite sides of the central 'plus' block and press again.

15 To make the unit at the top of the central 'plus' block, sew together units (O) and (M) making sure they are facing in the correct direction. Repeat to make the block at the bottom.

16 Press these units, then sew onto the top and bottom of the central 'plus' block and press again.

17 Sew the remaining eight flying geese in two rows of four. Press then sew one row at the top of the above unit and the other below, both with the flying geese facing inwards.

18 Sew piece (g) on the bottom of the block, and piece (h) on the top.

19 Sew one (i) piece on either side of the above unit and press.

17

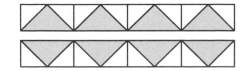

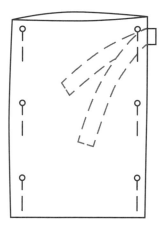

QUILTING AND MAKING UP THE COVER OUTER

20 Spray or pin baste the front and the back onto the pieces of wadding (batting) and quilt as desired (see Techniques: Hand Quilting). I used embroidery thread to hand quilt running stitch rows to highlight the units on the front, and three simple rows on the back.

21 Fold the ribbon tie in half and mark this halfway point.

22 Pin the front and back of the cover together with right sides facing, pinning the tie in place approximately 3½in from the top. Make sure the fold of the tie is facing outwards and the ends face inwards, lying between the right sides of the fabric.

23 Sew around the sides and bottom of the cover. Turn it right way out, pushing the corners out.

MAKING THE LINING

24 With right sides together, pin the lining pieces. Sew around the two long sides and bottom of the lining leaving a 5in gap along the bottom for turning. Leave inside out for now.

MAKING UP THE COVER

25 Push the cover outer inside the lining so that the right sides are facing.

26 Pin around the top, lining up the side seams and sew around.

27 Turn the cover the right way out by pushing the outer through the gap in the lining. Fold the open lining gap inwards and sew closed by hand or machine.

Breaking Rules

FINISHED SIZE: 80in x 80in

I decided to give the traditional log cabin quilt the wabi-sabi treatment. Not all the centre squares are the same size or colour, and while the strips all begin the same width, by the time the squares are trimmed they end up different. The joy in this quilt is anything goes! If you haven't got the correct length for the strips that doesn't matter – join two strips together. The result is a perfectly imperfect quilt… my favourite kind.

- -

Materials:

- 1½yds in total of fabric for the log cabin centres
- 6yds in total for the log cabin strips
- 5yds of fabric for backing
- ¾yd of fabric for binding
- 90in square of wadding (batting)
- Embroidery thread for hand quilting (optional)

CUTTING

1 Cut out the fabric as follows:

For the log cabin centres:

- Forty-nine squares, varying from 4in square to 7in square, using ½in increments

For the log cabin strips:

- 2½in wide strips. You'll trim these to the required length as you make the blocks

For the backing fabric:

- Two 2½yds x WOF rectangles

MAKING A LOG CABIN BLOCK

2 Take a centre square and measure the length. Cut the first log cabin strip to this length and sew onto one side of the square.

3 Press the seam away from the centre.

4 Cut two strips 2in longer than the previous strip. With the previous strip running along the top of the centre square, sew the next strip to the right-hand side of the block. Repeat with the next strip – you will sew strips around the block in this clockwise direction.

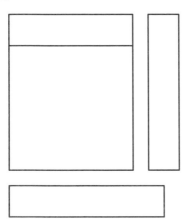

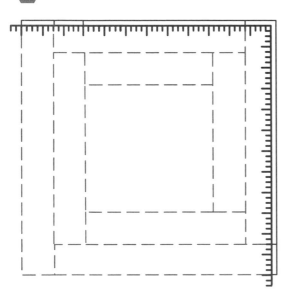

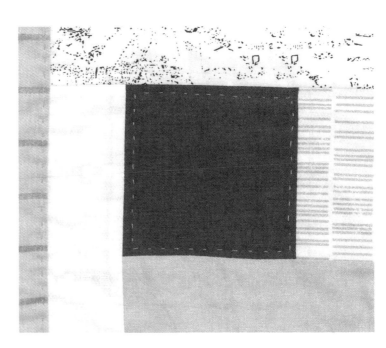

5 Continue adding pairs of strips 2in longer than the previous pair until the block is just over 12in square. You will be adding just one strip of the longest length to create a square.

6 The number of strips you add will depend on your starting square dimensions so make sure you measure the dimensions of your block as you go.

7 When you have reached 12in square (or just over) trim your block to exactly 12in x 12in. Your last round of strips may end up narrower than the others as you trim but that's fine; this only adds to the perfectly imperfect look of your quilt top!

8 Repeat to make a total of forty-nine blocks.

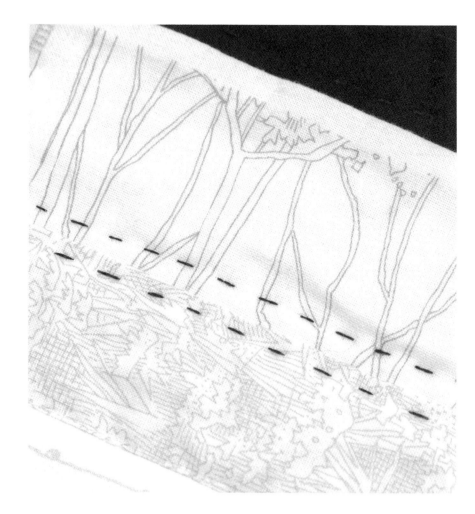

ASSEMBLING THE QUILT TOP

9 Lay out your blocks in seven rows of seven, and move these around until you are happy.

10 Sew each row of blocks together, then sew the seven rows together, pressing as you go.

QUILTING AND FINISHING

11 Sew the two pieces of backing fabric together along their long sides with a ½in seam allowance. Press the seam open.

12 Make a quilt sandwich with the backing fabric right side down, wadding (batting) and your pieced top right side up (see Techniques: Making a Quilt Sandwich).

13 Quilt with your preferred quilting method, whether this is hand quilted (see Techniques: Hand Quilting), machine quilted or another method of your choice. I machine quilted in the ditch along the block seams, then hand quilted detail in each individual block, mixing it up as I went.

14 Trim to 80in square and bind the quilt to finish, taking care to mitre the corners neatly (see Techniques: Binding Your Quilt).

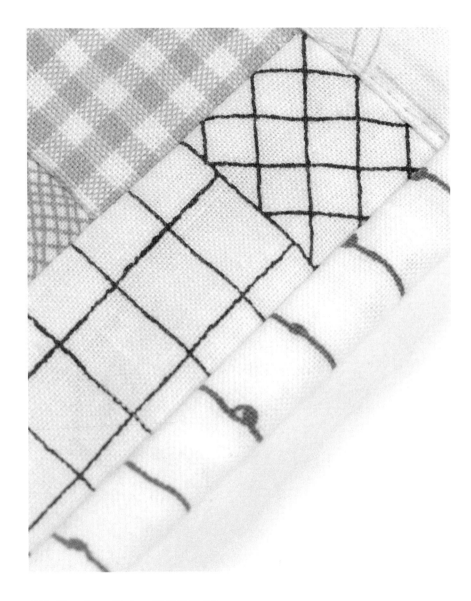

TEMPLATES

Download printable versions of these templates from:
http://ideas.sewandso.co.uk/patterns.

Picture Imperfect

Templates shown actual size

Templates shown actual size

Main motif

Sashiko
template

Circle
template

Circle motif (cut 4)

Flower motif (cut 4)

Hexagon Harmony

Templates shown actual size

1in hexagon templates

1in

TECHNIQUES

USEFUL INFORMATION

Here is some handy information to bear in mind as you use this book.

ABBREVIATIONS USED

- in – inches
- yd(s) – yard(s)
- HST(s) – Half Square Triangle(s)
- WOF – Width of Fabric (usually as cut from the bolt – 42in to 44in wide)
- EPP – English Paper Piecing

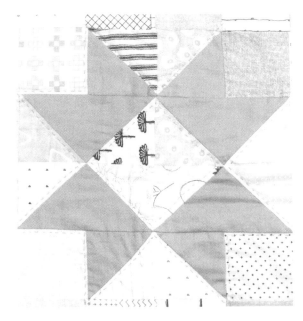

SEAM ALLOWANCES

Unless stated otherwise, seam allowances are ¼in. All fabric requirements have been given with this in mind. Because we are going for a perfectly imperfect vibe we don't need to be too fixated on our seams being wholly accurate. However, in order to accurately join pieced units and blocks, it's worth taking care at this stage.

PIECING UNITS

I've used half square triangles and flying geese in several of the projects. Here is how to make them, plus nifty tricks for making them in batches. The project will tell you how many units you need and which technique to use.

HALF SQUARE TRIANGLES (HSTs)

Half square triangles can be made in three ways, depending on how many you need. All three methods use the same principle of sewing ¼in away from specific lines and require some trimming. If you want all your HSTs to be different then the 'Sewing a Pair' method is best. If you require four or eight HSTs to be made from the same fabrics then there are two batch methods. The project will tell you which method to use, and give fabric dimensions accordingly.

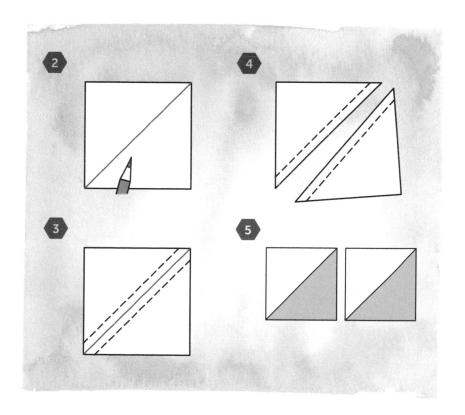

Sewing a Pair of HST Units

1 Take two fabric squares of the size as directed by the project and place right sides together, aligning the edges.

2 Use a fabric pencil to draw a diagonal line from corner to corner on the back of one square.

3 With right sides still facing, pin the squares together and sew a line ¼in away from both sides of the line.

4 Using a ruler and rotary cutter (see Tools & Materials), cut along the pencil line. Open up the two HSTs.

5 Press the seams to the darker fabric side and trim to the required size.

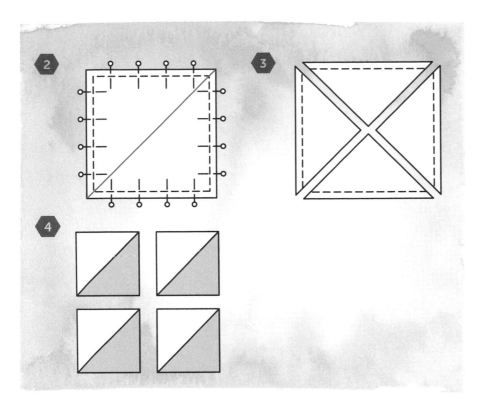

Sewing Four-At-a-Time HST Units

1 Take two fabric squares of the size directed by the project and place right sides together, aligning the edges.

2 Pin the two squares together and sew with a ¼in seam allowance around all four edges.

3 Remove the pins, and with a ruler and rotary cutter cut along both diagonals to yield four HST units.

4 Open up the four units, press the seams to the darker fabric side and trim to the required size.

Sewing Eight-At-a-Time HST Units

1 Take two fabric squares of the size as directed by the project and place right sides together, aligning the edges.

2 Use a fabric pencil to draw diagonal lines through the corners on the back of one of the squares.

3 With right sides facing, pin the squares together and sew ¼in away from both sides of both diagonal lines.

4 With a ruler and rotary cutter (see Tools & Materials) cut through the middle of the block horizontally and vertically, then cut along all the diagonal lines to yield eight HSTs.

5 Open up the eight units, press the seams to the darker fabric side and trim to the required size.

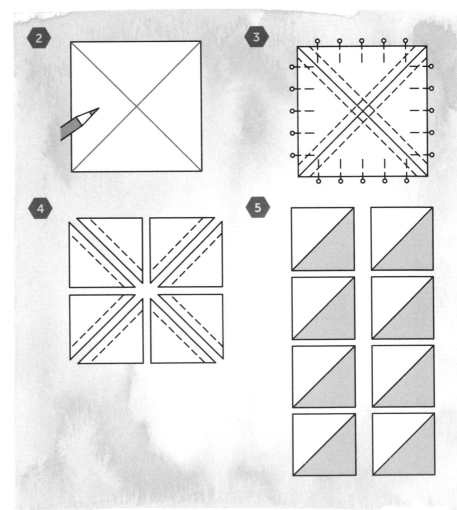

FLYING GEESE

Flying geese units can be made individually if you want each one to be different. If you want all of your units to be identical, and save time, use the Four-At-a-Time method.

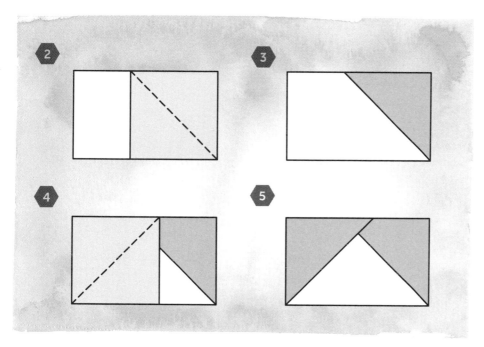

Sewing a Single Flying Geese Unit

1 Take two fabric squares and one fabric rectangle as directed by the project.

2 Use a fabric pencil to draw a diagonal line from corner to corner on the back of one of the squares. Pin this square, with right sides facing, onto the rectangle piece. Make sure the diagonal line is pointing from the top middle to the bottom corner.

3 Sew along this line and trim away the excess, i.e. the top triangle. Press the lower triangle back over the seam with the right side facing up

4 Repeat with the second square on the other corner.

5 You now have one flying geese unit. Trim to the required size.

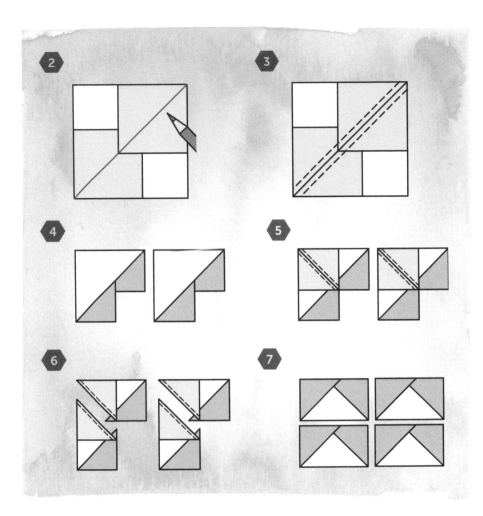

Sewing Four-At-a-Time Flying Geese Units

1 Cut one large fabric square and four small squares as directed by the project.

2 Take your large square and with right sides facing, pin a small square on opposite corners. Using a ruler and fabric pencil, draw a diagonal line from corner to corner.

3 Sew ¼in away from both sides of the line, then with a ruler and rotary cutter (see Tools & Materials) cut along the pencil line.

4 Press the seams open to the dark side of both units.

5 With a fabric pencil, draw a diagonal line on the back of the remaining two squares. Pin one of these onto each of the above units with the diagonal running from the corner to the middle. Sew ¼in away from both sides of these lines.

6 With a ruler and rotary cutter, cut along the pencil line of both units.

7 Press the seams open to the dark side of these four units.

8 Check the flying geese are the required measurements. If they need to be trimmed, align the centre point ¼in away from the edge, and at the same time make sure the bottom is trimmed to the diagonal line.

FINISHING OFF YOUR QUILT

All the quilts in the book are finished in the same way, sandwiched with wadding (batting) and sealed with a bound edge. The project instructions explain in detail how to make the quilt top, so here is what you need to do next.

MAKING A QUILT SANDWICH

Once you have made your quilt top, you need to layer it with wadding (batting) and the quilt backing. Start by laying your quilt backing onto the floor, or onto a large table, right side down. Smooth the backing flat and secure it in place with masking tape, ready for joining together by spray or pin basting.

Spray Basting

Spray basting is faster than pinning, but make sure the room is well ventilated while you are doing this.

1 Gently and evenly spray one side of the wadding (batting), then centre it on top of the wrong side of the prepared backing. Smooth the wadding (batting) from the centre outwards to eliminate wrinkles or bumps.

2 Spray all over the second side of the wadding (batting), and with the right side up, centre your quilt top on top of the wadding (batting). Again, smooth from the centre outwards.

Pin Basting

This is the traditional method of basting, joining the three layers of the sandwich together with safety pins or specially made basting pins.

1 Lay the wadding (batting) directly onto the prepared backing, centring and smoothing it out.

2 With the right side up, centre your pieced top on top of the wadding (batting) and again smooth from the centre outwards.

3 Use the pattern of the pieced top to help you plan a 'grid' for the pins

4 Work from the centre of the quilt outwards to allow for any movement as you pin and smooth. Make sure the pin goes through all three layers – top, wadding (batting) and backing. Place the pins 3in to 5in apart.

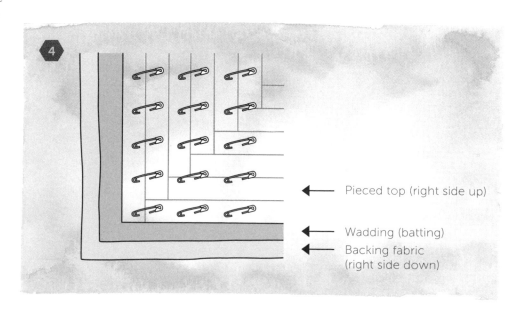

← Pieced top (right side up)

← Wadding (batting)
← Backing fabric (right side down)

STITCHING AND QUILTING

To secure layers of fabric and wadding (batting) together, and for decorative effect, hand stitching is the perfect wabi-sabi technique. The effect is charming and the process relaxing. Have fun selecting different colours of thread to blend, coordinate or contrast with your project.

Running Stitch

Running stitch technique is used to embellish many of the projects. Much of the inspiration behind this is the ancient Japanese technique of sashiko. This stitch was used to make repairs to clothing, both to mend and to strengthen the fabric, but in a way that was visible and decorative. There are many wonderful patterns that can be created, but I've kept it simple with straight rows of stitches, or gentle curves. I used Aurifil 12 cotton thread or Aurifil Lana wool thread.

The needle fills with stitches more easily when there is no wadding (batting). However, it's important to ensure stitches are neat and even when there is no piecing or wadding to disguise uneven stitch lengths.

1 Thread your needle with an arm's length of thread and make a small knot at the end.

2 Bring the needle up from the back of the fabric where you want to begin. If your stitched piece is already layered with backing fabric, give the thread a small tug to pull the knot through the backing where it's hidden between the layers.

3 Gather three or four stitches at a time on your needle as done in hand quilting (see Hand Quilting). You're aiming for stitches approximately ¼in in length, with a slightly shorter gap in between each one. This ensures a bold, decorative effect.

4 Continue stitching, following the pattern of the piecing or template, or moving freestyle across the surface.

5 To finish, tie off the thread in a small knot at the back of the work. If the work is already layered with its backing, refer to the technique for hand quilting before you tie the knot.

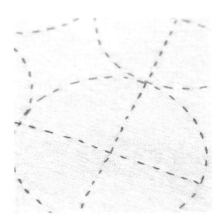  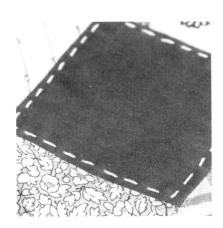

Hand Quilting

Choose a good quality, strong embroidery thread for your hand quilting, and preferably something that comes in a wide choice of colours to coordinate with your projects. I used Aurifil 12 cotton thread or Aurifil Lana wool thread for the hand quilting.

1 Thread your needle with 12in–18in of thread and make a small knot at the end. To hide this knot, put the needle into the quilt top just next to where you'll start stitching, and pull it through to the back to start your first stitch until the knot 'pops' through the fabric and is hidden beneath.

2 To make stitches through the thickness of the quilt sandwich, push the needle vertically through the layers to make the first stitch.

3 By rocking the needle in and out of the fabric, gather two or three stitches at a time before pulling the thread through the fabric. Make approximately four stitches per inch, making the space between the stitches the same width. Although this makes each stitch and space approximately ⅛in each, this is wabi-sabi so don't worry too much about it!

4 Work the stitches up to the edge of the quilt top, but not onto the wadding (batting) or backing.

5 The stitches should make a slight indent in the fabric to create the quilted effect. However don't pull too tight as the fabric will pucker.

6 When you come to the end of your length of thread, wind the thread around the needle twice and make a knot close to the surface. Insert the needle into the fabric and bring it back out 1in away, 'popping' the knot under the fabric as before. Cut the thread level with the surface and it will disappear beneath the fabric.

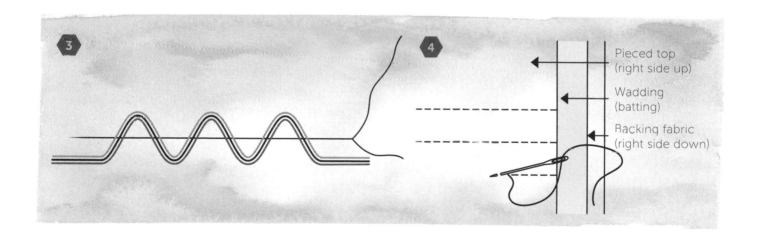

Pieced top (right side up)

Wadding (batting)

Backing fabric (right side down)

BINDING YOUR QUILT

Binding encases the raw edges of a quilt sandwich (or the raw edge of a piece of fabric if it's visible in a design). There are various way to make binding, but my instructions are based on cutting straight (as opposed to on the bias) and using a double fold. Attach binding to the front of the quilt by machine, then to the back by hand or by machine (but if hand quilting, I prefer to do it by hand as I don't want to see machine stitches on my hand finished quilt). It is a lovely way to sit and contemplate your finished project, having it on your lap while you slowly complete your quilt, stitch by stitch.

Squaring Up

After you have quilted, you need to trim away the excess fabric and wadding (batting) before binding. This gives you sharp, even sides with which to work. A square clear ruler as large as you can afford is best for this job.

1 Align your quilting ruler with one corner of the quilt top and trim from there. Trim away the excess wadding (batting) and quilt backing and as little of the quilt top as you can to square the sides.

2 Repeat all the way around the quilt. Make sure you put your ruler at right angles to the corners of the quilt to keep it squared up on each side. You may need to trim a bit more of the quilt front in order to do this.

Preparing the Binding

You will be creating continuous binding long enough to go around all four edges of the quilt. The materials list of the project will tell you how much fabric you need for this.

1 Cut the given fabric quantity into 2½in wide strips by the WOF.

2 To join the strips together, position the first two at right angles, with right sides together.

3 Sew diagonally across from top left to bottom right.

4 Sew all the strips together in this way, then trim the excess fabric with a ¼in seam allowance and press. Press the seams open.

5 The total length of the binding should equal the perimeter of your quilt plus at least 10in.

6 With wrong sides together, fold your length of binding in half lengthways and press.

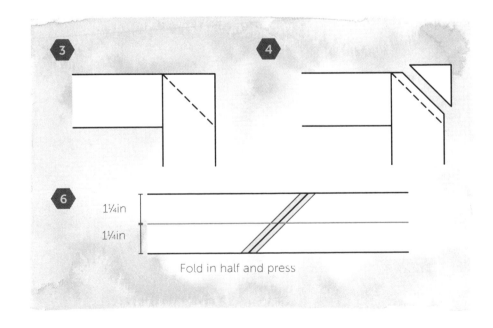

1¼in

1¼in

Fold in half and press

Attaching the Binding to Your Quilt

You will machine stitch the binding onto the front of the quilt and create neat mitred corners.
When the binding is folded to the back of the quilt, the machine stitches will be hidden.

1 Leaving a 5in excess of binding, and with the binding folded lengthways, align the raw edges of the binding with the edge of the quilt sandwich. Pin and sew with a ⅜in seam allowance. When you get ¼in away from a corner, backstitch to secure, then remove your quilt from under the needle.

2 To mitre the corner, turn the unsewn end of the binding up at right angles away from the quilt, then fold it back down to follow the second side of the quilt.

3 Pin this in place and start sewing along this second side, starting from the corner.

4 Continue around the other three corners and along the first side until you are about 5in away from the beginning. Backstitch in place and remove the quilt from under the needle.

5 Overlap the two binding ends and trim the excess so they overlap by just 2½in. Join these ends together in the same way you joined the strips to prepare the binding. Trim the excess, refold and finish sewing the binding to your quilt.

6 Fold the binding over to the back of the quilt, smoothing the mitred corners to create a neat diagonal fold. Pin in place and slip stitch the back of your binding in place.

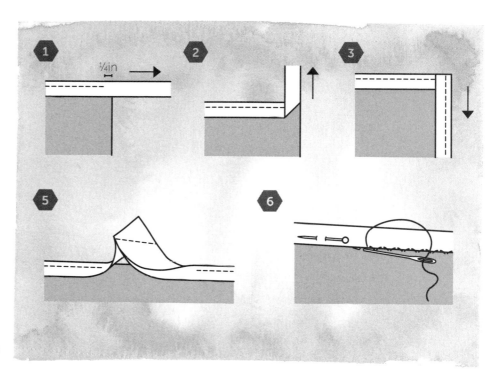

Binding a Raw Edge

On some projects such as cushion covers, you might want to bind the raw edges on the back of the cover. This is also a handy technique for adding a decorative edge or hiding the worn edge of an existing item.

1 Make the binding as described above. The length should match the raw edge being covered exactly.

2 Sew the binding to the wrong side then flip to the right side. In this case you might choose to also machine stitch this side too for a neat finish.

3 As the rest of the project is made up, the two raw edges of the binding will be hidden in the seam allowance.

ENGLISH PAPER PIECING (EPP)

This technique allows you to create geometric shapes with finished edges ready to be joined to other pieces or appliquéd down as embellishment. Paper templates are used, so ensure you have cut out all the templates required before you start (the project will tell you which templates you need, and how many).

1 Pin a template onto the wrong side of the fabric piece. The fabric should be approximately ¼in–½in larger than the template all round.

2 Fold the fabric around the template and finger-press for crisp edges. Tack (baste) in place using a needle and thread, taking care not to push the needle through the paper. (You should be able to remove the papers afterwards and use them again.)

3 Move the piece round as you tack (baste), folding and stitching each side by turn.

4 The fabric should completely encase the sides of the template with no raw edges showing at the sides or front.

5 Make the number and shapes required, then follow the project instructions for how to use them in your design.

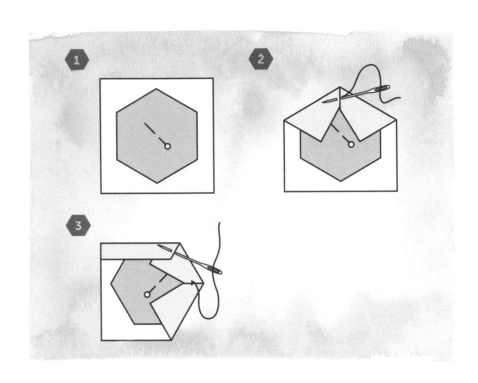

SUPPLIERS

Aurifil

www.aurifil.com

email: info@aurifil.com

tel: +39 0296 798833

Superior Egyptian cotton thread in a multitude of weights and colours.

Beyond Measure

www.shopbeyondmeasure.co.uk

email: grace@ shopbeyondmeasure.co.uk

tel: 07468 866834

Beautiful objects for the sewing room sourced and chosen by owner Grace from the UK and further afield.

Cloud 9 Fabrics

www.cloud9fabrics.com

email: info@cloud9fabrics.com

tel: +1 908 271 8200

Organic cotton fabrics printed with eco-responsible, low impact dyes that make beautiful fabrics to accompany sewing projects.

Ella Blue Fabrics

www.ellabluefabrics.com

email: info@ellabluefabrics.com

An Australian family-owned fabric house designing modern and fresh quilting and dressmaking fabric.

Ernest Wright & Son Ltd

www.ernestwright.co.uk

email: enquiries@ernestwright.co.uk

tel: 0114 2739977

The best haberdashery scissors about, handmade in Sheffield, UK.

Guthrie & Ghani

www.guthrie-ghani.co.uk

email: info@guthrie-ghani.co.uk

tel: 0121 449 8419

A fabric emporium and sewing school in Birmingham, UK, full of the most gorgeous and special fabrics, yarn and haberdashery.

M is for Make

www.misformake.co.uk

UK based online fabric shop offering a beautiful carefully chosen selection including cotton, linen and double gauze.

Miss Matatabi Fabric

https://shop.missmatatabi.com

Japanese based online fabric store offering a carefully handpicked selection of gorgeous hard to find Japanese textiles.

Oakshott

www.oakshottfabrics.com

tel: 01452 371571

100% ethically sourced shot cottons in an array of stunning vivid colours.

Robert Kaufman

www.robertkaufman.com

email: info@robertkaufman.com

tel: +1 310 538 3482

US family-run fabric manufacturer and supplier offering an extensive array of fabrics for quilting, dressmaking and home decor.

SewandSo

www.sewandso.co.uk

email: sales@sewandso.co.uk

tel: 0800 013 0150 (from within UK)

tel: +44 20 3808 6645 (from outside UK)

A brilliant range of fabric and threads for sewing and stitching.

The Village Haberdashery

www.thevillagehaberdashery.co.uk

email: info@ thevillagehaberdashery.co.uk

tel: +44 207 624 5494

London, UK based modern craft shop and class studio where you will find an inspiring collection of fabrics of all substrates.

Tierney Barden

www.tierneybarden.com

Beautiful hand dyed fabrics all made from natural dyes. Available in a variety of rich colours and substrates.

> To Matthew, who helped calm my night-time angst by talking through everything at ridiculous hours. x

ACKNOWLEDGEMENTS

First and biggest thanks go to my family, hubby Matthew and children Samuel, Noah and Ruby. You put up with me creating chaos all over our home and leaving your sewing repairs bottom of the heap. My extended family and friends have been equally supportive, always wanting to know how the book was going. I have to mention some people by name. My sister Sara starting each phone call with 'I know you are busy but...'; Jo and Lynne, my partners in crime at The Thread House, have been a valuable sounding board throughout; Cathi and Tierney – thank you for creating beautiful fabrics that made my projects shine and for your friendships across the waters; Jenni, Kay and Nim for coming over for an emergency hand quilting session.

Thank you to some very generous people who provided fabrics and notions for the book. Robert Kaufman and Aurifil, your support as ever is invaluable; Cloud 9 Fabrics, Ella Blue Fabrics, Ernest Wright & Son, Grace at Beyond Measure, and Oakshott, I appreciate your generosity. Lauren at Guthrie & Ghani, Kate at M is for Make, Frances at Miss Matatabi Fabric and Annie at The Village Haberdashery – your kindness and support in providing just the right fabrics is so appreciated.

A big thank you to the team at F&W Media, including Sarah, Jeni, Lorraine, Ali and Jason for sharing my vision for just how the book should look, and for your expertise in producing a book we are all very proud of. Jenny F-P, I was delighted to learn you were going to be editing the book. I knew I would be in safe hands.

Finally, thank you to every one of you who has bought my fabric, my previous book, been to my workshops or simply popped by on social media. I could not have done any of it without you.

ABOUT THE AUTHOR

Karen Lewis is a screen printer, fabric designer and quilter living in Leeds, West Yorkshire with her husband Matthew and three virtually grown up children Samuel, Noah and Ruby. Much adored Cockerpoo Scout has recently joined the clan and when she isn't knee deep in paint and fabric and designing for Robert Kaufman, Karen and Scout can be found around and about the fields by her house. Karen teaches printing and textiles at workshops around the UK and overseas, including Quiltcon and is one third of the UK based The Thread House with fellow quilters Lynne Goldsworthy and Jo Avery. You can find out more about Karen on her website karenlewistextiles.com.

INDEX

A SEWANDSO BOOK
© F&W Media International, Ltd 2018

SewandSo is an imprint of F&W Media International, Ltd
Pynes Hill Court, Pynes Hill, Exeter, EX2 5AZ, UK

F&W Media International, Ltd is a subsidiary of F+W Media, Inc
10151 Carver Road, Suite #200, Blue Ash, OH 45242, USA

Text and Designs © Karen Lewis 2018
Layout and Photography © F&W Media International, Ltd 2018

First published in the UK and USA in 2018

A catalogue record for this book is available from the British Library.

ISBN-13: 978-1-4463-0709-0 paperback
SRN: R7785 paperback

ISBN-13: 978-1-4463-7663-8 PDF
SRN: R7957 PDF

ISBN-13: 978-1-4463-7664-5 EPUB
SRN: R7956 EPUB

Printed in USA by LSC Communications for:
F&W Media International, Ltd
Pynes Hill Court, Pynes Hill, Exeter, EX2 5AZ, UK

10 9 8 7 6 5 4 3 2

Content Director: Ame Verso
Acquisitions Editor: Sarah Callard
Managing Editor: Jeni Hennah
Project Editor: Jenny Fox-Proverbs
Proofreader: Cheryl Brown
Design Manager: Lorraine Inglis
Designer: Ali Stark
Illustration: Kuo Kang Chen
Art Direction: Laura Seddon
Photographer: Jason Jenkins
Production Manager: Beverley Richardson

F&W Media publishes high quality books on a wide range of subjects.
For more great book ideas visit: www.sewandso.co.uk

Layout of the digital edition of this book may vary depending on reader hardware and display settings.